I0138039

The Sensitivity of the Spirit

The Sensitivity of the Spirit

R. T. Kendall

CHARISMA
HOUSE

THE SENSITIVITY OF THE SPIRIT by R. T. Kendall
Published by Charisma House
Charisma Media/Charisma House Book Group
600 Rinehart Road
Lake Mary, Florida 32746
www.charismahouse.com

This book or parts thereof may not be reproduced in any
form, stored in a retrieval system or transmitted in any form by
any means—electronic, mechanical, photocopy, recording or
otherwise—without prior written permission of the publisher,
except as provided by United States of America copyright law.

Unless otherwise noted, all Scripture quotations are from Holy
Bible, New International Version. Copyright © 1973, 1978, 1984,
International Bible Society. Used by permission.

Scripture quotations marked KJV are from the King James
Version of the Bible.

Cover design by Pat Theriault
Front cover photo by Pat Theriault

Copyright © 2002 by R. T. Kendall
All rights reserved

Library of Congress Catalog Card Number: 2001097452
International Standard Book Number: 9781636412108
E-book ISBN: 978-1-59979-850-9

Previously published in Great Britain as *Sensitivity of the Spirit*,
by Hodder and Stoughton, a division of Hodder Headline Ltd.,
ISBN 0-340-75628-4, copyright © 2000.

21 22 23 24 25 — 24 23 22 21 20

To Bob and Diane

CONTENTS

FOREWORD

R. T. Kendall deserves to be heard…and read. His years as the faithful pastor of the historic Westminister Chapel in London have won him credibility as a theologian and a thinker as well as respect as a preacher. As few men I have ever known at his intellectual level, he is incredibly open to the person and work of the Holy Spirit in an era when most folks feel that one position inevitably cancels the other. What a rare find to discover a man whose intellect is ablaze with the Spirit! Such a man is necessarily daring to expose himself and his people to cutting-edge ministries wherever they are found. Such daring has put R. T. Kendall squarely in the midst of a move of God that is not apt to wane any time soon.

He knows what it is to see the healing of God in his own life and that of his family. It has also touched his church family. He is not afraid to venture into areas studiously avoided by most men in order to walk less trodden paths.

Faithful to the unique tradition he inherited from Martyn Lloyd-Jones before him and G. Campbell Morgan before Lloyd-Jones, R. T. has been faithful to the Word; he respects it greatly and preaches it tirelessly.

I have said these things about the author of *The Sensitivity of the Spirit* because I believe most of us who buy books read the author before we read his books. I would want to read any work by R. T. Kendall because I have read the man.

This volume is such that my response is, "How I wish

it was written a half-century ago when I was in the early morning of my ministry." Because many of these issues were not shared with me by anyone when I was young, I was tossed about by many winds, particularly regarding the doctrine of the Holy Spirit. It would surely have been different had I been exposed to this reference.

No field of study today is more of a theological minefield than that relating to the Third Person of the Trinity. Through no fault of his own, the One who has been sent to bring unity to the church seems to be a point of much disunity. The understanding exhibited in this book would serve to pour much oil on severely troubled waters. Many believers today have chosen to avoid the study altogether. An unfortunate decision! Others have boldly charged in with more fire than light, throwing caution to the wind. Another unfortunate decision!

No study demands more precision and fortitude than that regarding the Holy Spirit. In this study R. T. exhibits both. Such topics as the Spirit's sensitivity, the loss of our sensitivity, the mysterious silence of God, the seeming absence of God, the road of repentance and recovering the anointing are sensibly and satisfyingly explored to the benefit of all of us who read this work.

The chapter on the pigeon and the dove (chapter eight) will likely remain a standard in the annals of spiritual literature for years to come (as classic, perhaps, as the turkey and the eagle). It makes for an unforgettable and edifying illustration.

May God use this work to bring revival to the church everywhere by unifying the Word streams with the Spirit streams throughout the world. I predict for this volume a wide and greatly helped readership.

—JACK TAYLOR
DIMENSIONS MINISTRIES
MELBOURNE, FLORIDA

PREFACE

This book is the product of at least four episodes in my life over many years. The first is a sermon preached by Joe Jones, my first roommate at Trevecca Nazarene College in Nashville, Tennessee. I heard him preach a sermon that he called "The Lost Christ," based upon Luke 2:41–42. This is the first time I gave any thought to this passage.

The second event was hearing Dr. Hywel Jones read John 1:32–33 in Westminster Chapel. He happened to be in the service, and I asked him if he would read the Scripture I would be preaching from. Either it was his Welsh accent or the Spirit of God (I think the latter), but the way he pronounced "remain" went so deep in me that I thought about it for many, many days. I don't believe there have been many times in my life when the mere reading of Scripture has had such a profound impact upon me. This book would not have been written had not Hywel read John 1:32–33 as he did.

The third development was when I addressed a group of Elim ministers in Northern Ireland in 1999. I gave some talks based upon *The Anointing: Yesterday, Today, Tomorrow*. One of the ministers, Rev. Walker Gorman, approached me to say, "I have a story that fits with what you have been teaching, and I think it could interest you." It was the account of Sandy and Bernice, which begins chapter 1. I cannot imagine this book without that amazing story. Thank you, Walker.

Finally, my wife, Louise, and I visited Pete and Melissa Cantrell in Ada, Oklahoma, later in 1999. What I learned from Pete about doves and pigeons has given this book such a flavor that I hate to think how impoverished it would be without this information. Talk about providence! Thank you, Pete!

I therefore believe that I have been prepared to write what follows for quite a long time. I only pray that it will bless you and bring honor and glory to the name of our Lord Jesus Christ.

My thanks to my editor at Charisma House, Barbara Dycus, and to a host of friends, especially Lyndon Bowring, Colin Dye and Rob Parsons for their suggestions. Thanks also to Anne Williams, who read my manuscript.

When I thought of who might write the Foreword, I kept thinking of Jack Taylor. I asked him to write it, and he kindly has done so, for which I am thankful.

This book is dedicated to Bob and Diane Ferguson, who now reside in Mandeville, Louisiana. They have been the dearest of friends for over twenty-five years. A book dedicated to them is long overdue. God bless you both, Bob and Diane.

—R. T. KENDALL

Every year his parents went to Jerusalem for the Feast of the Passover. When he was twelve years old, they went up to the Feast, according to the custom. After the Feast was over, while his parents were returning home, the boy Jesus stayed behind in Jerusalem, but they were unaware of it. Thinking he was in their company, they traveled on for a day. Then they began looking for him among their relatives and friends. When they did not find him, they went back to Jerusalem to look for him.

After three days they found him in the temple courts, sitting among the teachers, listening to them and asking them questions. Everyone who heard him was amazed at his understanding and his answers. When his parents saw him, they were astonished. His mother said to him, "Son, why have you treated us like this? Your father and I have been anxiously searching for you."

"Why were you searching for me?" he asked. "Didn't you know I had to be in my Father's house?" But they did not understand what he was saying to them. Then he went down to Nazareth with them and was obedient to them. But his mother treasured all these things in her heart. And Jesus grew in wisdom and stature, and in favor with God and men.

—Luke 2:41–52

INTRODUCTION

> My greatest fear is that God would remove His hand
> from me.
>
> —BILLY GRAHAM

I was converted when I was six—on April 5, 1941. I
began studying the Bible earnestly in my teens and felt
called to the preaching ministry when I was nineteen.
In over fifty years of studying the Bible, one truth has
alarmed me more than any other. You might think it has
to do with standing before God at the final judgment.
But, surprising as it may seem, it isn't that. The truth
that alarms me most is the possibility of grieving or
quenching the Holy Spirit without knowing it—the
painless way in which the anointing can be lifted from
me. When this occurs, because I know nothing whatever
at first, I carry on as though nothing has happened. As
we will see in the life of Samson, it is possible for one

who has experienced the precious anointing of the Holy Spirit to swiftly, painlessly, lose that anointing. I can displease the Lord and feel nothing. It is very possible that I could spend years doing what I presumed was God's will—preaching, teaching, witnessing and being involved in church work—when God was hardly present in my efforts at all. I may even have the applause and respect of people the whole time, and they not have a clue I have moved ahead of Jesus.

It is a great mystery of the anointing of which one may be unaware—even though it is working most powerfully. On the other hand, one also may not be conscious that it has been lifted! When Moses came down from Mount Sinai, "he was not aware that his face was radiant" (Exod. 34:29). Yet Samson, who could tear a lion apart with his bare hands, was as weak as a kitten when the anointing left him—but he was unconscious of this until he tried to do what had seemed so natural the day before. (See Judges 14:6; 16:20–22.) The supernatural often seems natural to the anointed man or woman.

ANOINTED BY THE HOLY SPIRIT

The anointing is the power of the Holy Spirit—the special presence of God. And yet the anointing can be manifested in any number of ways. Every Christian therefore has an anointing. But this anointing is applied sovereignly by the Spirit "as he determines" (1 Cor. 12:11). Not every Christian has the same specific application of the anointing—we are all different. John's use of the word *anointing* illustrates this: He first states, "But you have an anointing from the Holy One, and all of you know the truth" (1 John 2:20). Then John expands his teaching by continuing, "As for you, the anointing you received from him remains in you, and you do not need anyone to teach you. But as his anointing teaches you about all things and as that anointing is real, not counterfeit—just as it has taught you, remain in him" (v. 27). These verses refer to the anointing of the Holy Spirit, which is present in every believer—uniquely applied by God's Holy Spirit.

Samson's anointing manifested itself in unusual physical strength. One time this anointing was manifested when the Philistines bound Samson with two new ropes. We read of Samson's response:

> The Spirit of the LORD came upon him in power. The ropes on his arms became like charred flax, and the bindings dropped from his hands. Finding a fresh jawbone of a donkey, he grabbed it and struck down a thousand men.
>
> —JUDGES 15:14–15

However, Samson had a particular weakness, one that had to do with women. He fell in love with Delilah—who was part of a setup by the Philistines. They used her to discover the secret of his great strength. In a moment of great weakness, he finally told her everything: "If my head were shaved, my strength would leave me, and I would become as weak as any other man" (Judg. 16:17). While Samson was sleeping, Delilah instructed that his head be shaved. Promptly "his strength left him" (v. 19). With no warning of any kind, his anointing—and with it his great physical strength—was gone!

> Then she called, "Samson, the Philistines are upon you!" He awoke from his sleep and thought, "I'll go out as before and shake myself free." *But he did not know that the LORD had left him.*
>
> —JUDGES 16:20, EMPHASIS ADDED

Samson therefore felt nothing at the time. He only discovered the loss of his strength when it was too late.

3

"Then the Philistines seized him, gouged out his eyes and took him down to Gaza. Binding him with bronze shackles, they set him to grinding in the prison" (v. 21).

For all I know there may have been an unconscious diminishing of Samson's anointing during the time he foolishly allowed Delilah to keep probing him for his secret: "With such nagging she prodded him day after day until he was tired to death" (v. 16). What we do know is that when his head was shaved his strength utterly left him. He lost the anointing—and didn't know it…at first.

Samson is not the only person to whom this has happened. There have been servants of Christ—some with high profiles—who, through compromise, lost their anointing but felt no loss at the time. Some were being powerfully used in large, visible ministries—a fact they often took as proof of God's approval and anointing. But they gave in to sexual temptations and felt nothing as the anointing left them. Billy Graham has said that the devil seems to get 75 percent of God's best servants through sexual temptation.

The account of Samson is an Old Testament example of what the apostle Paul calls *grieving the Spirit*: "And do not grieve the Holy Spirit of God, with whom you were sealed for the day of redemption" (Eph. 4:30). When the Holy Spirit is grieved, the anointing lifts. We usually feel nothing at the time. It isn't until some time later that we notice we have carried on out of habit or through the momentum of a natural gift.

THE PRESENCE OF GOD

But it is a New Testament story that became my main inspiration for writing this—the account of Joseph and Mary moving ahead of Jesus and leaving Him behind in Jerusalem.

Every year his parents went to Jerusalem for the Feast of the Passover. When he was twelve years old, they went up to the Feast, according to the custom. After the Feast was over, while his parents were returning home, the boy Jesus stayed behind in Jerusalem, but they were unaware of it. Thinking he was in their company, they traveled on for a day. Then they began looking for him among their relatives and friends. When they did not find him, they went back to Jerusalem to look for him.

After three days they found him in the temple courts, sitting among the teachers, listening to them and asking them questions. Everyone who heard him was amazed at his understanding and his answers. When his parents saw him, they were astonished. His mother said to him, "Son, why have you treated us like this? Your father and I have been anxiously searching for you."

"Why were you searching for me?" he asked. "Didn't you know I had to be in my Father's house?" But they did not understand what he was saying to them. Then he went down to Nazareth with them and was obedient to them. But his mother treasured all these things in her heart. And Jesus grew in wisdom and stature, and in favor with God and men.

—Luke 2:41–52

In this story I know we are talking about Jesus—not the Holy Spirit. In fact, we are looking at young Jesus while He lived here on earth with His earthly parents. Nevertheless, this illustration from the life of Jesus illustrates the way in which the sovereign Holy Spirit may test our sensitivity to Him by not moving with us when we choose to carry on with our plans.

The occasion was not only the observance of the Feast of Passover, but it was also the *Bar Mitzvah* of Jesus.

This event is when a Jewish boy is recognized formally as becoming a man. Although from birth Jesus was God as though He were not man, and man as though He were not God, Jesus was now being truly authenticated as the God-man—especially by Joseph and Mary, who knew the facts.

There are theological implications here that have to do with when Jesus was truly conscious of who He was and what His mission was. No doubt He fully realized these things at His baptism. (See Matthew 3:17.) But suffice it to say that on this occasion, as John Calvin put it, Jesus was given a single "practice round" of what He would develop into. Here was twelve-year-old Jesus, sitting among the rabbinical teachers like one of them, astonishing all who heard Him with His understanding, questions and answers. What a moment it must have been.

But Joseph and Mary missed it. Apparently, the dialogue with Jesus and the teachers in the temple continued for three days—all without the knowledge of Joseph and Mary. I fancy that when we get to heaven we will see a video replay of the whole three days! All this was happening because God was sovereignly at work. Jesus was doing His Father's business. It was a "practice round" of what He would later say about Himself: "I tell you the truth, the Son can do nothing by himself; he can do only what he sees His Father doing, because whatever the Father does the Son also does" (John 5:19). Or, as He would also put it, "By myself I can do nothing; I judge only as I hear, and my judgment is just, for I seek not to please myself but him who sent me" (v. 30).

What a pity that Joseph and Mary missed it. The focus of the entire story pivots on one striking phrase: *"Thinking he was in their company*, they traveled on for a day" (Luke 2:44, emphasis added). When the Feast was over, Joseph and Mary returned home. Jesus stayed behind, but "they were unaware of it" (v. 43). In other words, they sincerely thought Jesus was right there with them. Why? They presumed He would adjust to their thinking and plans. After all, it was—as far as they were concerned—time to go home. They did not see a need of adjusting to Him. But He chose to stay behind.

This reminds me of the words of the Episcopal rector who shocked many Christians by his comment on a national radio broadcast: "If the Holy Spirit were totally withdrawn from the church today, 90 percent of the work of the church would go on as if nothing had happened." The same thing can happen to you or me.

Joseph and Mary moved on as if nothing had happened. Unaware that Jesus had stayed behind, they sincerely thought He was with them.

Joseph and Mary went to the Feast of Passover every year. No doubt they attended other annual feasts as well, since they wanted to be obedient to the Law (Luke 2:39). They probably sang the Psalms of Ascent with the pilgrims as they ascended the holy hill of Jerusalem. (See Psalms 120–134.) They knew the territory well.

Luke's account, which he no doubt learned from Mary (Luke 2:51), is our only information about Jesus between the accounts of His miraculous birth and His public appearance on the scene at the age of thirty (Luke 3:23). We all would love to know more, but we must conclude that God has given us all we need.

But why did Luke include this account of Joseph and Mary taking twelve-year-old Jesus to Jerusalem? Why is this event important for us?

1. One reason is what partly inspires the theme of this book. In this book we will see how to develop a sensitivity to the Spirit—which is only possible as we become aware of the sensitivity of the Spirit. This

illustration from the life of Jesus shows how we can run ahead of God as a result of not focusing on His Son and adjusting to the sensitivity of the Spirit. We, like Joseph and Mary, may think the whole time that Jesus is with us, only to discover that He is hardly with us at all. Therefore we must learn to adjust to Him—and not expect Him to adjust to us.

2. The immediate presence of Jesus is like the anointing—the immediate and direct witness of the Spirit of God. This example shows one of the differences between God's omnipresence and His special presence. Theologians often speak of the attributes of God, three of which are the big *O's*—His omnipotence (He is all-powerful), His omniscience (He knows everything) and His omnipresence (He is everywhere). Indeed, listen to the psalmist:

> Where can I go from your Spirit?
> Where can I flee from your presence?
> If I go up to the heavens, you are there;
> if I make my bed in the depths, you
> are there.
> If I rise on the wings of the dawn,
> if I settle on the far side of the sea,
> even there your hand will guide me,
> your right hand will hold me fast.
> —PSALM 139:7–10

Therefore it is quite wrong in one sense to say that God is not with us. After all, God said, "Never will I leave you; never will I forsake you" (Heb. 13:5). We can never get outside His omnipresence. But we can lose the *special*

8

presence of God—the anointing. It happened to Samson. However, God had not totally left Samson. He got his anointing back in the end. (See Judges 16:30.)

3. If we discover that we have moved ahead of God and have left Him behind, we must go looking for Him. That is what Joseph and Mary had to do. "When they did not find him, they went back to Jerusalem to look for him" (Luke 2:45).

4. Once we have lost God's special presence, we can only find Him by initially returning to the place where we lost Him. By place, I do not necessarily mean a literal, physical place as in a building or even a geographical location. I mean recalling what it was like when He was consciously present, remembering the circumstances that may have contributed to His staying behind and reassessing and repenting of the self-justifying (but ill-advised) ways we proceeded, thinking He was in our company. We only find Him by discovering where He is and by coming to terms with what He is doing. Joseph and Mary had to go back to Jerusalem—where they lost Jesus. It wasn't until they returned to Jerusalem that they finally found Him and saw what He was up to.

5. This account demonstrates that it is easier to lose the anointing than it is to get it back. After a day's journey Joseph and Mary realized they had left Jerusalem without Jesus. It was another three days before they found Him. "After three days they found him in the temple courts,

sitting among the teachers, listening to them and asking them questions" (Luke 2:46).

6. We miss seeing the next sphere of God's activity when we move on without Him. He does not promise to adjust to us. He carries on without us, but He still continues to work. "My Father is always at his work … and I, too, am working" (John 5:17). It is a sober reminder that heaven doesn't shut down merely because we are not directly involved ourselves. Joseph and Mary could not conceive of Jesus doing anything extraordinary without them, but He did. He asked them, "Didn't you know I had to be in my Father's house?" (Luke 2:49).

We can learn a lot about God's sovereignty and about human responsibility from this story. Had Jesus not stayed behind—or had Joseph and Mary remained with Him—Luke would not have had this story to tell.

I believe the Bible categorically affirms the sovereign grace of God in salvation. We are chosen apart from works (2 Tim. 1:9), saved apart from works (Eph. 2:8–9) and kept apart from works (Rom. 8:28–39). We are loved with an everlasting love (Jer. 31:3). There is nothing we can do to make God love us more—and we can do nothing to cause Him to love us less. We are secure and kept by the sheer grace of God.

But that is not all we need to know when it comes to living the Christian life and pleasing God. God puts us on our honor to "guard the good deposit that was entrusted to you" (2 Tim. 1:14). The verse continues by reminding us of how we do it—"guard it with the help of the Holy Spirit who lives in us." That deposit is the anointing, the special presence of God. We can lose this anointing without forfeiting being saved. God takes the responsibility for our making it to heaven, but He warns us that the anointing is a trust here below that must be carefully guarded by us with the help of the Spirit.

I write this book to examine ways by which we may hopefully avoid the mistake Joseph and Mary made. What they did by moving on without Jesus seems understandable to any parent. When she realized Jesus was missing, Mary probably felt embarrassed. She knew in her heart that they had not been as careful as they should have been. So I write this book to see if we can discover hints from this account that will show us how not to move ahead without the Lord. It is a mistake I have made myself hundreds of times.

Of course, we don't know all of the reasons Jesus stayed behind in Jerusalem without telling His parents. I suspect it was mainly because He knew it was what He was called to do. But I think He did it for them as well. We don't know all the facts about why Joseph and Mary headed for Galilee without their Son. From our "big picture" spiritual perspective, it certainly seemed inevitable at that time. Jesus simply had something to do that transcended their human knowledge. In much the same way, our propensity to grieve or quench the Spirit may also seem unavoidable at first.

Therefore, I do not write this book with the view that we can reach the place this side of heaven where we will never again move ahead of the Holy Spirit. I don't want to be too hard on Joseph and Mary, or too hard on myself. Neither do I want you to feel any false guilt if you find yourself in the position of leaving the Spirit behind as Joseph and Mary left Jesus. After all, "if we claim to be without sin, we deceive ourselves and the truth is not in us" (1 John 1:8).

We all need the rebuke of Ecclesiastes 7:16 from time to time: "Do not be overrighteous, neither be overwise—why destroy yourself?" As Solomon put it, "There is no one who does not sin" (2 Chron. 6:36). Simon Peter honestly thought he loved the Lord Jesus more than Jesus' other followers loved Him. Yet he was the very one who denied knowing Jesus when the pressure was on. (See Matthew 26:69–75.) At the end of the day, we are going to cause the heavenly Dove to fly away from time to time. Nobody's perfect. As Calvin put it, "In every saint there is something reprehensible." Is not this part of the meaning of the psalmist's words, "To all perfection I see a limit" (Ps. 119:96)?

I must therefore bring an extremely important caution. There may be a person with an "overly sensitive" conscience who carries this principle of not grieving the Spirit too far and finds himself or herself in an unnecessary bondage. For example, some people may be so fearful of grieving the Spirit that they are afraid to do *anything* without a minute-by-minute sense of clear guidance. They worry about which pair of shoes to wear, which tie to put on or whether to read a newspaper. They cannot turn on the television without "guidance." They are fearful of any entertainment, fearful of laughing at a joke or spending money in a good restaurant. The irony is, such a bondage equally grieves the Spirit! For where the Spirit of the Lord is, there is liberty (2 Cor. 3:17). One legacy of the Reformation is the doctrine of Christian liberty. "It is for freedom that Christ has set us free. Stand firm, then, and do not let yourselves be burdened again by a yoke of slavery" (Gal. 5:1).

A healthy fear of grieving the Spirit should not lead you to being afraid to enjoy life to the full, to laugh uproariously with friends or to make common-sense decisions day and night. God is not unreasonable. His commands are never "burdensome" (1 John 5:3). Bond-

12

age to rules is not what this book is about.

On the other hand, I must eagerly desire all of God I can possibly have. I would love it if God would increase my anointing each day I live. I want to learn ways by which I can adjust to the special presence of God.

Moving ahead without the Lord is an easy thing to do. We've all done it. But when we do so, we miss what God is doing elsewhere while we are, as it were, on our way to Galilee. We can avoid such a thing happening by learning to adjust to the Dove, which we will take a look at as we move into the next chapter.

CHAPTER ONE

The Sensitivity of the Heavenly Dove

The cooing of doves is heard in our land.

—SONG OF SOLOMON 2:12

15

A few years ago a British couple, Sandy and Bernice, accepted a call from their denomination to be missionaries in Israel. A house was provided for them near Jerusalem. After they moved into their new home, they noticed that a dove had come to live in the eaves of the house. They were honored to be living near Jerusalem and were particularly thrilled to have the dove come and live there. They considered it to be something of a seal of approval from the Lord, a confirmation that they were in the right place.

Sandy noticed an unsettling pattern in the dove's behavior, however. Every time a door slammed shut—or if there was a lot of noise in the house, or if they raised their voices—the dove would be disturbed and flutter off, sometimes not returning for some time. This worried Sandy, as he felt they were in danger of frightening the dove off permanently. With this in mind, he brought up the matter to his wife.

"Have you noticed that every time there is a lot of noise, or if we slam the door, the dove flies away?" he asked.

"Yes, and it makes me feel sad. I am afraid the dove will fly away and never come back," she replied.

"Well," said Sandy, "Either the dove will adjust his behavior to us, or if we really want to make sure we never lose him, we will have to adjust our behavior to the dove."

Watching that dove was a daily reminder to that precious couple of the similar lessons believers need to learn about our heavenly Dove, the Holy Spirit. It changed their lives forever.

THE HOLY SPIRIT DESCENDED LIKE A DOVE

When Jesus was baptized, He saw the Holy Spirit "descending like a dove and lighting on him" (Matt. 3:16). John the Baptist saw this as well and gave this testimony:

> I saw the Spirit come down from heaven as a dove and *remain* on him. I would not have known him, except that the one who sent me to baptize with water told me, "The man on whom you see the Spirit come down and *remain* is he who will baptize with the Holy Spirit."
>
> —JOHN 1:32–33, EMPHASIS ADDED

The more I have learned about the person of the Holy Spirit and the nature of a turtledove, the more extraordinary I find John's account. First, it is unusual—probably unprecedented—for a dove ever to alight voluntarily on a human being. But for the dove to remain is quite astonishing indeed. I don't know that our heavenly Father chose the dove as one of the first symbols in the New Testament for the Holy Spirit because of John the Baptist's familiarity with doves and their behavior. But I do know that the dove's coming down and remaining on Jesus told John all he needed to know at the time—"this is the Son of God" (John 1:34).

Obviously, the important word in John's account is *remain*. The Holy Spirit remained on Jesus. From time to time the Holy Spirit comes on me, but I'm afraid that sometimes He doesn't stay long. Dr. Martyn Lloyd-Jones was fond of quoting one of the Puritans who said, "The Holy Spirit comes by foot but leaves by horseback." This shows how sensitive the Holy Spirit is and how easy it is to grieve Him.

However, when He does come down, His conscious presence is wonderful. There is no more peaceful, blissful moment than when the heavenly Dove descends on me. There is not only peace when the Dove is present, but also presence of mind. Clear thinking. Courage and confidence. A feeling that God is in complete control. No need to panic—not even a fear of panic. As the psalmist says, "No fear of bad news" (Ps. 112:7). Although it is nearly impossible to describe such an experience, one verse of the hymn "Like a River Glorious" comes close:

> Hidden in the hollow of His blessed hand,
> Never foe can follow, never traitor stand;
> Not a surge of worry, not a shade of care,
> Not a blast of hurry touch the spirit there.[1]

THE SPIRIT DOVE—NOT
THE SPIRIT PIGEON

But why doesn't it last? The dove, especially the turtledove, is apparently a very shy, even hypersensitive bird. You can feed the pigeons in your city park, but probably not a turtledove. I doubt a dove like that ever comes near most busy city regions.

Although pigeons and doves both belong to the same order of birds—the *Columbidae*—the Bible makes a distinction between pigeons and doves (Lev. 12:8). Scientifically, the turtledove belongs to the genus *Streptopelia turtur*. According to Leviticus 12:8, either a dove or pigeon was acceptable for sacrifice. When Joseph and Mary presented Jesus for consecration in the temple shortly after His birth, they brought a sacrificial offering, but it is not known whether they brought a pigeon or a dove. (See Luke 2:24.) In much the same way, a lamb or goat was an acceptable sacrificial offering. (See Leviticus 3.) They are different, but look very alike in many ways.

The Bible does not say that the Spirit came down from heaven as a pigeon. There would probably have been nothing unusual about a pigeon descending on an individual—or even remaining.

Shortly after we moved to England in 1973, we came into London to feed the pigeons in Trafalgar Square. I have a photograph of our son T. R., who was seven years old at the time, with four pigeons on each arm and one on his head! It would seem that such is out of the question when it comes to a turtledove. We now live in central London. Every spring we have to come up with a new method to get rid of the pigeons that perch by our bedroom window, making guttural noises that wake us up too early in the morning. Louise has tried opening the window and shooing them away with a mop or broom handle. But these pigeons seem impervious to any punishment we can administer to them. They are a terrible nuisance.

I decided to investigate pigeons and doves. Despite what

18

the encyclopedias say, I knew there must be *some* differences—at least in temperament—between pigeons and doves. But I did not have the evidence or experience to prove it. Moreover, I was quite certain that Sandy and Bernice would not scare a pigeon away by a slammed door or heated argument inside. A pigeon—at least the pigeons of Trafalgar Square—would adjust to nearly any situation, but almost certainly a turtledove would not.

An unexpected invitation came our way while we were in America in August 1999. Our old and dear friend Pete Cantrell from Oklahoma, whom I quoted in *The Anointing: Yesterday, Today, Tomorrow*, arranged for me to preach where he goes to church in Ada, Oklahoma.[2] After Louise and I arrived, Pete wanted to show me his pigeons! I had not known until then that he has raised pigeons and turtledoves all his life! Pete is a Cherokee Indian and inherited a love for doves. His middle name is Grayson, named after the Grayson dove.

I couldn't believe it! I told him virtually everything I have written above and that I was confused over the supposed similarity between pigeons and doves. I have talked with some of the top experts on doves and pigeons on both sides of the Atlantic. They all insist that there is virtually no difference between pigeons and doves—unless, however, one is comparing a pigeon to a turtledove.

There are many kinds of pigeons and many kinds of doves. But according to Pete Cantrell, the turtledove is different. Pete made this observation: "I sometimes question whether turtledoves should be in the same family because a pigeon has a very good homing instinct—but a turtledove has none." Pete was speaking out of fifty years of experience in raising doves and pigeons, during which time he had observed them carefully.[3] He made the following observations:

19

1. Turtledoves never fight; pigeons fight with each other all the time. Peter told me that the turtledoves he raises are always peaceful and quiet. Their soft cooing is very beautiful and reassuring. On the other hand, pigeons are belligerent, noisy and anything but tranquil.

2. Turtledoves can't stand noise; pigeons don't mind noise.

3. Turtledoves are afraid of humans; pigeons aren't afraid of people.

4. Turtledoves are not territorial, that is, they do not defend a particular location; pigeons are very territorial and will even bully one another for a special place to perch.

5. Turtledoves cannot be trained or domesticated; pigeons, having a homing instinct, can be trained. Peter assured me, "I could put a red box in the center of New York City and train a pigeon to come to that box."

6. Once let out of a cage, turtledoves will never return unless there is no other source of food. Pete told me, "I once released fifty white turtledoves, thinking they would at least return for food. Not one came back. Friends phoned from all over Ada saying, 'Some of your doves are in our back yard.'" I watched Pete let a dozen pigeons out of their cage. They soared. As soon as he called to them, they returned to him at once. Pete's explanation helps us to understand the illustration of the dove Noah sent out from the ark: "But the dove could find no place

20

to set its feet because there was water over all the surface of the earth; so it returned to Noah in the ark. He reached out his hand and took the dove and brought it back to himself in the ark" (Gen. 8:9). The dove returned a second time with an olive leaf, but when the waters receded, the dove "did not return to him" (vv. 11–12).

7. A turtledove will mate with only one other dove. "Doves mate for life," says Pete, "but pigeons will sometimes have more than one mate."

At the end of our discussion about pigeons and turtledoves, Pete added, "A pigeon could never be the symbol of the Holy Spirit. Can you imagine a love song or a poem about the loud, boisterous pigeon?"

Any analogy can be pressed too far, and there is a danger of oversimplification in these illustrations and comparisons between pigeons and doves. There are many kinds of pigeons, many kinds of doves, and there is even more than one kind of turtledove. I do not wish to enter into a controversy with anyone! I do, however, believe that there are some visible and temperamental differences between the pigeons most of us know as pigeons and the turtledove, which is likely to be the dove symbolizing the Holy Spirit.[4]

When I was a student at Southern Baptist Theological Seminary in Louisville, Kentucky, I took a course in archaeology, which included a trip to Israel. One day as I walked toward the Western Wall (known as the "Wailing Wall"), an Israeli explained to me that once in a while you see a dove perched in one of the crevices of the Wall. As I looked at the Wall, I thought I was privileged to see such a sight! I took a photograph and included it as part of

21

my research project. But my balloon was punctured. My professor gently asked me to take another look. To my chagrin—it was a not a dove, but a pigeon! Perhaps a dove occasionally visits the Wailing Wall. But not that day.

Long seen as a symbol of peace, the harmless and gentle dove has already been designated by God as a symbol of the Holy Spirit. Jesus described a dove as "innocent" (Matt. 10:16; cf. "harmless" in the King James Version). The word used in Matthew comes from the Greek word *akeraios*. It is a word the ancients understood as meaning "pure or moral innocence; that which is in its original state of intactness." The turtledove, which thrives in the Middle East, would likely have been the dove of which the Bible speaks.

A fruit of the Spirit is "gentleness" (Gal. 5:23). Paul urged, "Let your gentleness be evident to all" (Phil. 4:5). He taught us that "the wisdom that is from above is first pure, then peaceable, gentle, and easy to be entreated, full of mercy and good fruits, without partiality, and without hypocrisy" (James 3:17, KJV). Those are the characteristics that are to be a part of our lives when the heavenly Dove is present.

I will never forget how humbled and embarrassed I was when I realized that I had not noticed that it was but a *pigeon* I had photographed at the Western Wall in Jerusalem. The suggestion the Israeli made about a dove had preconditioned my thinking. It had not crossed my mind that it could be a pigeon! The power of suggestion shaped my expectancy to such an extent that I thought I had pulled off a real coup for my research project.

PIGEON RELIGION

I wonder how often many of us have confused a pigeon for a dove at a spiritual level. We may hastily assume that the Dove has come, but a more objective examination might just show that it was a pigeon! Such a possibility has given me a new phrase—"pigeon religion."

On the same evening that Pete Cantrell explained the differences between turtledoves and pigeons to me, he turned on the TV to a religious program as we sat together in his living room. During that summer I had watched that program occasionally. As I listened to the claims being broadcast as the gifted TV preacher pumped the viewing audiences for financial support, I thought of our earlier discussion. I pray I am not being insensitive to the Holy Spirit, but I fear that so much today purports to be the presence of the Spirit—but in reality it is nothing more than pigeon religion.

It is my view that the genuine presence of the Holy Spirit is not as common as we may want to believe. It is also my fear that many of us have run slipshod over this matter and have forgotten that the Holy Spirit is a very, very sensitive person.

I know that I have been very guilty in this area. For instance, there have been times when I have joined in conversations with some who appear to feel no great anguish when speaking disparagingly of others. I have done some things—and not done others—that I later realized have grieved the Spirit. We all claim to want God's blessing on us—and even take strong public stands for the truth! But often there seems missing a real conscientiousness with regard to grieving the Spirit by attitudes and words. It is as if we think our official positions or titles exempt us from having to watch what we say. The sober truth is, God will not bend the rules for any of us, whatever our position may be.

It seems to me that this is a neglected emphasis in our theology and talk about the Holy Spirit. If I am correct, it would explain the lack of real power in our churches and in our personal lives. What if, when we get to heaven and look back on all our claims to the power of God, we learn that it was not the Dove among us at all, but one who looks so much like the Dove?

The dove is not the only symbol of the Holy Spirit in the Bible. Any analogy or comparison can be taken too far; however, I write this book for more than one purpose. I do want to try and fill a gap long overdue in our knowledge of the Holy Spirit. But I also believe there may be a *link* between the dove and other symbols of the Spirit such as fire, water, oil and wind. If the New Testament depicts Jesus with the dove remaining upon Him, what does this have to say to us? What is our identity as Christians? If we are truly to be like Jesus, is it not right to want to imitate Him in this way as well? (See Philippians 2:5–11.) If I am to be today's man or tomorrow's man—and make sure I am not yesterday's man—should I not want to ensure my anointing by focusing not only on the winds and fire, but also upon the sensitivity of the Spirit?

Of course we want the fire of the Spirit to be a part of our lives. But we also must respect the Spirit as a person of dignity and honor, and we must want *to know* Him—as opposed *to using* Him for our own goals. Knowing Him will cause us to hunger for His fire.

> Thou Christ of burning, cleansing flame,
> Send the fire!
> Thy blood-bought gift today we claim,
> Send the fire!
> Look down and see this waiting host,
> Give us the promised Holy Ghost.
> We want another Pentecost,
> Send the fire![5]

A SENSITIVE SPIRIT

Yes, we long to experience the fire as well as a mighty rushing wind in our church. But I believe that the way to power and more anointing is by being more sensitive to the Holy Spirit. I suspect that the Dove is the link to the fire.

The word *sensitivity* has two meanings. In essence, one meaning is "the capacity of being easily hurt." The other meaning is "the capacity for being aware of the needs and emotions of others." For some, having the capacity of being easily hurt may suggest a weakness in one's personality. We have all known people with whom we have to "walk on eggshells" to avoid hurting their feelings.

The second meaning, being sensitive to another's feelings, is a strength. We all need to develop in this area.

But when we speak of the sensitivity of the Holy Spirit, we must refer to *both* of these meanings. We may or may not think these qualities are very attractive in the Holy Spirit's personality, but like it or not, the Holy Spirit is like a turtledove—and flutters away where peace does not prevail. However, the Holy Spirit is equally sensitive to *our* feelings. The Holy Spirit is a gentleman.

There are two main truths I want this book to make clear. The first relates to the *sensitivity of the Holy Spirit*. This refers to His passive feelings. It refers to how sensitive He is when He is grieved. It is this aspect of His personality that causes the Dove to fly away. If we can tune in to the sensitivity of the Spirit, we learn what grieves Him, how to avoid grieving Him and how we must adjust to Him if we want His intimate company.

The second truth is the importance of developing a *sensitivity to the Spirit*. We must be tuned in to His active will, or voice. If we develop a sensitivity to the Spirit, we will hear Him when He speaks and thus avoid quenching the Spirit. In that way we can see the glory of God manifested in our lives and, hopefully, in the church.

THE HOLY SPIRIT'S PERSONALITY

The Holy Spirit is the third Person of the Godhead, just as Jesus is the second Person (John 1:1). We must never make the mistake of calling Him "it." This does not imply that either the Son or the Spirit is less divine than the Father. This description of the Godhead provides us with a human way of attempting to understand the concept of three persons in the Trinity. Just as Jesus is a person, so too the Holy Spirit is a person. Jesus has a personality. When He walked on earth, His disciples knew the sound of His voice and the color of His skin, hair and eyes. They knew how tall He was and exactly what He looked like. They knew His personality as He expressed it to them. For example, because He had the Spirit without limit, He would have perfectly manifested all the fruit of the Spirit. (See John 3:34.)

That the Holy Spirit descended and *remained* on Jesus tells us as much about Jesus as it does the Holy Spirit. The Holy Spirit was at home with Jesus. They were mutually adjusted to each other. Jesus carried no bitterness or hate, no grudges, panic or spirit of vindictiveness to drive away the gentle Spirit. Described by Matthew as "gentle and humble in heart," Jesus did not quarrel or cry out (Matt. 11:29). Yet "a bruised reed he will not break" (Matt. 12:20). He never struck out to hurt another.

Even when Jesus was confronted by the temple guards, who were responding to the religious leaders' instructions to arrest Jesus and bring Him before their court, He displayed an anointing and presence that caused the temple guards to hesitate. When the religious leaders demanded to know why the guards had failed to arrest Jesus, they declared, "No one ever spoke the way this man does" (John 7:46).

What can we learn about the Holy Spirit's personality?

THE SPIRIT CAN BE GRIEVED.

The apostle Paul admonished us, "And do not grieve the Holy Spirit of God, with whom you were sealed for the day of redemption" (Eph. 4:30). The Holy Spirit has feelings, and we can hurt His feelings when we grieve Him by the things we do. The Greek word translated "grieve" (*lupeo*) comes from *lupee*, which means "pain" or "sorrow." It is the opposite of joy.

We know from the apostle Paul that the Holy Spirit can also be quenched. In Paul's words, "Do not put out the Spirit's fire" (1 Thess. 5:19). The words *put out* come from the Greek word *shennumi*, which basically means "to quench." In the ancient Greek world it referred generally to extinguishing fire or burning objects. On the Day of Pentecost, the Holy Spirit came to the people gathered in the upper room as what seemed to be "tongues of fire" (Acts 2:3). Paul's warning not to quench the Spirit can only mean that sometimes the Spirit's fire can be put out. It is possible that such a quenching of the Spirit was the reason Jesus refused to perform miracles in Capernaum. Matthew 13:58 tells us that Jesus did not do many miracles there "because of their lack of faith." Implicit in this verse is the idea of quenching the fire of the Spirit as He moves in supernatural demonstrations of His power.

It is hard to know the difference between the Holy Spirit being grieved and being quenched. But there are nuances of understanding we can discover. *Grieving the Spirit* refers to actions of ours that hinder the Spirit from being Himself—from *being* what He could be *in us*. On the other hand, *quenching the Spirit* refers to actions of ours that hinder the Spirit from *doing* what He could do *through us*.

When He is *ungrieved* in us we will manifest His personality—defined in Galatians 5:22–23 as "fruit of the Spirit." These characteristics of the Spirit's personal-

27

ity include love, joy, peace, patience, kindness, goodness, faithfulness, gentleness and self-control. If we have not grieved the Spirit *in us*, we will also demonstrate these characteristics—just as Jesus demonstrated them.

When He is *unquenched* in us we may well manifest His power, perhaps through the expressions of the gifts of the Spirit. (See 1 Corinthians 12:8–10.)

There is no doubt that the capabilities of being grieved and being quenched overlap. Therefore this distinction should not be pressed too far, for they are similar in some ways. I suspect there has been a tendency for some, however, to be more concerned with *quenching* the Spirit because there is a desire to see His power (through signs and wonders). In some ways *grieving* the Spirit focuses more on Christlikeness. There has been a disproportionate interest in the gifts of the Spirit among some Christians. Some of us seem to want *power* more than *purity*—signs and wonders more than gentleness and graciousness, which are the forgotten anointing.

The anointing must be the totality of all that the Spirit is and is able to do. We must want to exemplify the personality of Jesus as much as to demonstrate His power. It seems to me that we must begin from within. That is, we must experience the Holy Spirit within— *ungrieved* in our private lives—before we can anticipate an outward demonstration of His power. God is sovereign, and He can overrule this progression whenever He wants to do so. But if we expect the dove of the Spirit to *remain*, it is surely essential that all we *are* does nothing to cause the Dove to flutter away.

I fear that neglecting this aspect of the sensitivity *of* the Holy Spirit's personality has resulted in the church's tendency to move on without Jesus, believing the whole time that He is still with us—when He is not. We have taken Him for granted. It seems not to have crossed

28

our minds that He, as a person, has a dignity of His own—He wants to be consulted, honored and *recognized* before we proceed.

What is needed, then, is a sensitivity *to* the Spirit. This means a sensitivity to His ways and—may it please God—to an immediate awareness of His *absence* should He withdraw to any degree. How quickly we recognize His absence is probably a fairly good test as to how well acquainted we are with Him. "They have not known my ways," said an offended Holy Spirit:

> So, as the Holy Spirit says:
> "Today, if you hear his voice,
>   do not harden your hearts
> as you did in the rebellion,
>   during the time of testing in the desert,
> where your fathers tested and tried me
>   and for forty years saw what I did.
> That is why I was angry with that generation,
>   and I said, 'Their hearts are always going astray,
>   and they have not known my ways.'
> So I declared on oath in my anger,
>   'They shall never enter my rest.'"
>
> —HEBREWS 3:7–11, EMPHASIS ADDED

But does this teaching make the Holy Spirit vulnerable to the charge of being capricious? Under no circumstances does it do this. He may appear that way from our point of view. But God always has a reason for what He does. He promised Moses, "I will have mercy on whom I will have mercy, and I will have compassion on whom I will have compassion" (Exod. 33:19). The Holy Spirit always mirrors the unity of the Godhead. Even though "the wind blows wherever it pleases" (Jesus' reference to the Spirit in John 3:8), the Spirit never does anything "on his own" (John 16:13). He therefore

29

reflects the will of the Father. The psalmist spoke of the *second* Person of the Trinity, "Kiss the Son, lest he be angry and you be destroyed in your way, for *his wrath can flare up in a moment.* Blessed are all who take refuge in him" (Ps. 2:12, emphasis added). Likewise, the Holy Spirit can be grieved suddenly—but never without reason. We must lower our voices and adjust to Him if it is the anointing we want. In part, this explains what is meant by "knowing His ways."

LEARNING TO KNOW HIS WAYS

I almost blush to admit that I was in the ministry for many years before this aspect of the Holy Spirit began to influence me. I had a "sound" doctrine of the Holy Spirit, but I fear it was largely soteriological, that is, mainly it had to do with applying the teaching of salvation. In other words, my doctrine of the Spirit was chiefly understood as the Holy Spirit's applying the gospel. If the Holy Spirit does not apply the good news that Jesus paid our debt on the cross, no one will be converted. Jesus also had a sound soteriological doctrine of the Holy Spirit, and He proved that by saying, "No one can come to me unless the Father who sent me draws him" (John 6:44). Only the Holy Spirit opens people's eyes and hearts.

One day I began to recall my experience of driving in my car. One Monday morning, on October 31, 1955, I was on my way to Trevecca Nazarene College in Nashville, Tennessee.[6] The glory of the Lord filled the car, and my heart, mind and life were instantaneously changed. This came as an immediate and direct manifestation of the Spirit. It was not a case of the gospel merely being applied—the Holy Spirit came in very clearly and noticeably as well. It was *so* powerful. The person of Jesus was literally more real to me than was anybody around me.

30

This glow of experience began to diminish in time. Years later my weekly visits to Dr. Martyn Lloyd-Jones at his home in Ealing, England, during 1977 to 1981 gave me a hunger and thirst to experience again the precious intimacy of God's presence. I used to talk about it with Dr. Lloyd-Jones. Sound doctrine simply wasn't enough—I wanted more. It was during those days that I first sensed how easy it was to grieve the Spirit.

I tried so hard to get everything right! I began to pray more. But if anyone—even in my own family—disturbed me when I was praying, I became very annoyed. As a result, instead of God being impressed with my efforts, the Dove fluttered away. Never mind that I was trying to please God—He would not bend the rules for me even if my motive was to keep from grieving Him. Through countless experiences like this, I have learned this fact: The Dove will not adjust to me; I must adjust to Him. And, I quickly add, *it isn't easy*.

I would go so far as to say that the easiest thing in the world to do is to grieve the Holy Spirit. Our anger, grudge-bearing or resentments come so naturally. Right after Paul spoke in Ephesians 4:30 of the possibility of grieving the Spirit, the very next thing he said was this:

> Get rid of all bitterness, rage and anger, brawling and
> slander, along with every form of malice. Be kind and
> compassionate to one another, forgiving each other,
> just as in Christ God forgave you.
>
> —Ephesians 4:31–32

GET RID OF BITTERNESS.

Bitterness is at the head of the list. Bitterness, or resentment, is one of the chief ways we grieve the Holy Spirit. Sadly, resentment always seems justifiable at the moment it surfaces. We often do not realize *at the time* that we are grieving the Spirit. He quietly flutters away

31

with no announcement or fanfare.

Whether He leaves because of our bitterness or because of something else, it often isn't until some time later that we realize He's gone. As we read earlier in the illustration of Samson, when he told the closely guarded secret of his strength to Delilah, "he did not know that the Lord had left him" (Judg. 16:20).

When the Spirit departs like this, it doesn't mean we have lost our salvation. Paul said, "And do not grieve the Holy Spirit of God, with whom you were *sealed* for the day of redemption" (Eph. 4:30, emphasis added). Nothing could be clearer than that! At the end of his life, Samson got his old anointing back and accomplished more "when he died than while he lived" (Judg. 16:30). Bitterness is not the only way we can grieve the Spirit, but it is at the top of Paul's list in Ephesians 4.

Avoid immorality.

Satan's chief strategy is to get us to grieve the Spirit, whether by sexual immorality or a bitter attitude. The devil knows God's ways—and ours. When we grieve the Spirit, we force God to treat us like an enemy. In James 4:4 we read, "You adulterous people, don't you know that friendship with the world is hatred toward God? Anyone who chooses to be a friend of the world becomes an enemy of God."

That is exactly what Satan wants. If he can cause us to grieve the Spirit—by working through any weakness we may have—he wins a battle. Satan worked in this way in ancient Israel through the influence of Balaam and Balak. Israel began to sin and consequently incurred God's wrath (Rev. 2:14). For this reason the devil, who knows each of us backward and forward, watches day and night for an opportunity to lure us to grieve the Spirit.

HIS DIMINISHING PRESENCE

After my experience with the awesome presence of the Spirit in my car that Monday morning in 1955, I began to lose that sense of the intimate presence of God. There may have been a gradual if not unconscious diminishing of the sense of His presence, of that I can't be sure. But I do remember how I became aware that I had completely lost this intimacy. It was in August of 1956.

I had always thought—and still do—that I have the best and most godly dad in the world. But I was not prepared for his reaction to my "Damascus Road" experience in my car. It was not the experience to which he objected. But he was unhappy with the theology to which it led me. My adjusted theology did not cohere with the doctrines of the denomination of which I had been a part. In my efforts to explain my experience, I lost it. I will never forget how distraught I was at the time. Most distressing was the realization that came later verifying that the Dove had completely flown away. It is easier to lose the anointing than it is to get it back.

Many years ago I started on a pilgrimage to recover that old sense of the ungrieved Spirit powerfully inside me. It has returned in slow stages. I believe it has been a slow process because the way back must be a return *to* the anointing—not a return *of* the anointing. In the following chapters we will see that one must move on and be willing not to have everything exactly as we once knew it. Someone once put it this way: You can step out of a flowing stream, but you can never step back in at the same place. Seldom is everything exactly as it once was. We must adjust to what God has for us now—not then.

Sometime during the summer of 1956 the Lord Jesus must have "stayed behind." But I was initially unaware of it—as were Joseph and Mary (Luke 2:43). I kept on going, thinking He was in my company. At first I did

33

not want to admit I had lost that special anointing. But eventually I came to terms with the truth. Little was the same as before.

I looked in my comfort zone to find what I lost, but with no joy. Like Joseph and Mary, I have had to go back to my equivalent of Jerusalem. It has been a long journey, but one worth traveling. This book is about the journey.

CHAPTER TWO

Adjusting to the Heavenly Dove

Return, O holy Dove! Return,
Sweet messenger of rest!
I hate the sins that made Thee mourn
And drove Thee from my breast.
—WILLIAM COWPER (1731–1800)

The presence of an earthly dove dramatically altered Sandy and Bernice's lives. They made a conscious, deliberate choice to adjust to this earthly dove, and their lives were never the same again.

How much more important is the company of the heavenly Dove in our lives, whose personality is far more sensitive than that of an earthly dove. Your own life too can be wonderfully altered overnight—and you will never be the same—if you consciously and deliberately choose to adjust to the Dove. He will manifest Himself in surprising ways. The consequences are incalculable.

But why won't the Dove adjust to us? The truth is, He could—if He wanted to. In the story of the way God dealt with Jonah after Ninevah was not destroyed we see an example of this. When Jonah brought the news of impending destruction to the people of Ninevah, he put his reputation on the line, declaring, "Forty more days and Ninevah will be overturned" (Jon. 3:4). When they heard his message, the people repented. And God responded to their repentance: "When God saw what they did and how they turned from their evil ways, he had compassion and did not bring upon them the destruction he had threatened" (v. 10).

God's response should have pleased any man of God, but not Jonah. He was "greatly displeased and became angry" (Jon. 4:1). His anger was sufficient to drive the Dove away.

But despite Jonah's anger and resentment, God maintained communion with him. God spoke to Jonah, asking, "Have you any right to be angry?" (v. 4). Then God continued by explaining His actions with the worm and the vine. It is always God's sovereign prerogative to determine what happens next.

God has been gracious to all of us at times. "For he knows how we are formed, he remembers that we are dust" (Ps. 103:14). Generally speaking, however, God tends to recall the Dove away from us when we are filled with bitterness, hold grudges, refuse to forgive or do not have our sexual appetites under control. He requires us to adjust to the Dove, which means adjusting to the sovereignty and standard of the gentle Spirit.

Jonathan Edwards taught us that the task of every generation is to discover the direction in which the Sovereign Redeemer is moving, then to move in that direction. Joseph and Mary missed what the Lord was up to because they failed to determine Jesus' direction. Jesus stayed behind in Jerusalem, but they were not aware of it.

No doubt they felt that if Jesus made an important decision, they would be the first to be told. After all, they *were* special. They, if anyone, would be informed of what God would do next!

Adjusting to the Dove must often be done without knowing *why* the Spirit is leading in a particular manner. When the angel told Philip to head toward the desert, at the time he had no idea why (Acts 8:26). He demonstrated a highly developed sensitivity to God's voice. It was not a case of Philip's being spoken to through the written Word or being gripped by a sermon. God spoke to him immediately and directly.

Why doesn't this sort of thing happen today? It should. After all, as Dr. Lloyd-Jones used to say, "The Bible was not given to replace direct revelation; it was given to correct abuses." By *abuses* he meant going against Scripture—God's final and ultimate revelation. But many of us are so loath to listen to God when He speaks immediately and directly to us that there are seldom abuses (mistakes we can make) to correct! Should God be pleased to speak in such a manner, it would also mean that much is going on behind the scenes—in the heavenlies. He trusts us to obey without knowing all of the reasons why He gives a particular word. In the same way, then, Jesus stayed behind in Jerusalem and did not explain the reason to His parents.

If we want God to speak directly to us today as He did to Philip, it follows that we will want the honor that comes from God alone and not that which comes from people (John 5:44). This may include keeping quiet about such immediate and direct communication from God, for this sort of thing could easily go to our heads. That is probably why God doesn't dispense such intimacy very widely. But it is something He *would* do with us if we could keep to ourselves such two-way communication with Him (Ps. 25:14).

37

SOMETIMES WE MUST STAY

Receiving honor from God has many requirements. We must be willing to appear foolish and stupid to ourselves and to others by obeying God's immediate voice. This will cause us to be vulnerable to criticism and correction from others around us. The criticism may be just or unjust. If it is unjust, we must show a sweet spirit. If it is a fair criticism, we must accept correction. Defensiveness against valid criticism grieves the Spirit—it shows resentment. Maintaining a teachable spirit and graciousness toward our critics will help ensure that the Dove remains.

I suspect that staying behind was no small decision for Jesus to make. This was the first "practice round" of what He would develop into. Perhaps it was also the first crucial test in Jesus' life as to whether He would listen exclusively to His Father. He too would need to develop a sensitivity to the Spirit. Undoubtedly it was the Father who beckoned Jesus to stay in Jerusalem. Therefore it was a real test of Jesus' obedience. As we must, Jesus learned obedience through suffering (Heb. 5:8). Always, part of the suffering is to put God first rather than those closest to us.

As a twelve-year-old boy, this must have been very difficult for Jesus. But it was a lesson He learned well. Some twenty years later, when told that His mother and brothers were outside the place where He was ministering and that they were looking for Him, He would respond, "Here are my mother and my brothers! Whoever does God's will is my brother and sister and mother" (Mark 3:32–35). For all I know, that may not have been easy for Him to say even twenty years later. But imagine the feelings of twelve-year-old Jesus as He learned to stay behind and listen only to His Father God.

Sometimes it is God's will for us just to *stay*. We may

want to move on—but God may want us to stay. We may say, "It's time to get moving. Let's get the show on the road."

But God says, "Stay. In quietness and trust is your strength" (Isa. 30:15).

We may be bored and feel like saying, "The Feast is over. Let's go home." That's what Joseph and Mary were saying. But God told His Son, "Stay behind."

The ancient people of Israel had to learn this lesson. They had to learn to take their cues only from the visible glory of God—the pillar of fire by night and the cloud by day.

> In all the travels of the Israelites, whenever the cloud *lifted* from above the tabernacle, they would set out; but if the *cloud did not lift, they did not set out*—until the day it lifted. So the cloud of the LORD was over the tabernacle by day, and fire was in the cloud by night, in the sight of all the house of Israel during all their travels.
>
> —EXODUS 40:36–38, EMPHASIS ADDED

Israel was locked into this manner of direct guidance from God. They could only move when the cloud lifted. If the cloud did not lift, they stayed. No matter how tedious and tasteless that particular place in the wilderness might have been, they had to "stay put" until they were released to move on. The cloud did not adjust to the Israelites; they had to adjust to the cloud. It often takes as much courage to stay as it does to move. It may take even more faith sometimes to remain where you are than to explore a new geographical area.

It may not be mere boredom, however, that tempts one to move on. Sometimes it is opposition. Paul went into Corinth to preach the gospel. His custom was to offer the gospel to Jews first (Rom. 1:16). This he did in Corinth.

"But when the Jews opposed Paul and became abusive, he shook out his clothes in protest and said to them, 'Your blood be on your own heads! I am clear of my responsibility. From now on I will go to the Gentiles'" (Acts 18:6). Paul left the synagogue where he had been preaching and went next door. He had some spectacular conversions (vv. 7–8). But the persecution was so fierce that Paul *wanted* to move on. "One night the Lord spoke to Paul in a vision: 'Do not be afraid; keep on speaking, do not be silent. For I am with you, and no one is going to attack and harm you, because I have many people in this city'" (vv. 9–10). As a result, Paul stayed for a year and a half longer. A great church was formed, and we all have the benefit of 1 and 2 Corinthians as a result. All because Paul stayed.

Whenever God says, "Stay," it is with a definite purpose. We will never be sorry when we remain where we are, even though we may not know the reasons at the time, if God says we must.

I continually hear of more and more people who leave secular work for Christian work. They assume their new sphere of work will be "spiritual." A young man recently called a friend of mine and said, "I can't wait to get out of my office and get into Christian work. I'm so tired of office politics." My friend, who has spent many years in a parachurch organization, was amused at the naiveté of that young man.

LEARNING TO ADJUST TO THE FATHER'S WILL

Jesus may not have known entirely why He was constrained to remain behind when Joseph and Mary were moving on. But He adjusted to the Father's will regardless.

Louise and I came to England in 1973 for me to do

research at Oxford. Our son T. R. was seven; Melissa was three. Initially we agreed to stay for two years, the minimum stay then required by Oxford University to get a research degree. Those were hard days. I felt over my head from the first day. Here I was in that august seat of learning, having come from the hills of Kentucky—a state not known for its high educational standards. And I was trying to adjust to the British system, to which nearly everyone around me was well acquainted.

On top of that, our children struggled with school and relationship issues. On many days, T. R. would come home crying and ask me, "How long will we be staying over here?"

"Not long," I assured him. "One day we are going home."

The two years at Oxford had to be extended to three, then another three months. It was during those last three months that I was invited to preach at Westminster Chapel. We began our ministry there in February 1977. In May 1977 we were called to stay permanently. One of the hardest things I ever had to do was to look T. R. in the eyes when he said, "Daddy, you said we were going home." That was nearly twenty-three years ago, yet as I write these lines, I still feel the pain to this day. The cloud has refused to lift after all those years.

But God's sovereign prerogative to stay is never without its reason—or benefits. Part of the reason Jesus stayed behind in Jerusalem was because He had more to learn in Jerusalem—and more to teach others as well. He amazed the teachers of the Law with His questions and answers. It was a way of learning for Jesus. Dr. Michael Eaton, a close friend of mine, reckons that twelve-year-old Jesus was zealous to discover everything He could about God and His will. He once told me, "Although Jesus was the Son of God, He was also a genuine man.

He did not know everything all in one instant. He had to learn and grow. So He took every opportunity to learn more of the things of God."

One day in the future, possibly, some of these very teachers—or certainly men like them—would be Jesus' chief antagonists. This time with them while He was still a boy enabled Jesus to see what they were like and to learn how their minds worked. Probably at that time they exhibited no hostility, just a friendly atmosphere for Jesus. The teachers were only fascinated that a twelve-year-old Jewish boy could hold their attention.

But this was a time of preparation for Jesus. Very likely He mulled over their questions and answers, discovering how they viewed the Law and what their messianic expectations were. It would be another eighteen years before He would be confronted by the likes of them. No doubt years later He reflected back on *all* that happened during those days of preparation in the temple courts. Sadly, it would be teachers of the Law who helped lead the way to His death years later (Luke 23:10).

LEARN TO LISTEN TO THE SPIRIT'S VOICE.

This was training for Jesus to learn to *listen*. Three days later, Mary and Joseph found Him "listening to them" (Luke 2:46). Listening is an art. Few people truly learn to listen. We love to talk more than to listen. I know I do. I find listening hard. A good listener, like a wise judge, listens to all the evidence before making a decision. A doctor who makes a diagnosis before he or she hears the patient's whole story is not a good doctor. Jesus turned out to be the greatest listener that ever was. He still listens. He is our great High Priest who is able to sympathize with our weaknesses because He listens (Heb. 4:15).

LEARN TO ASK THE RIGHT QUESTIONS.

The time in the temple was also preparation for Jesus

to learn to ask the right questions. He was not only listening to the teachers in the temple, but He was also "asking them questions" (Luke 2:46). Knowing how to ask the right questions reflects acute discernment and wisdom. Years later Jesus would manifest an unparalleled brilliance in asking questions. "Which is easier: to say, 'Your sins are forgiven,' or to say, 'Get up and walk'?" (Luke 5:23). Or how does one answer this question: "What good is it for a man to gain the whole world, yet forfeit his soul?" (Mark 8:36)? Jesus could initiate a discussion by raising questions that showed the folly of His opponents' views.

> While the Pharisees were gathered together, Jesus asked them, "What do you think about the Christ? Whose son is he?"
> "The son of David," they replied.
> He said to them, "How is it then that David, speaking by the Spirit, calls him 'Lord'? For he says, 'The Lord said to my Lord: "Sit at my right hand until I put your enemies under your feet."' If then David calls him 'Lord,' how can he be his son?" No one could say a word in reply, and from that day on no one dared to ask him any more questions.
>
> —MATTHEW 22:41–46

Staying behind in Jerusalem was a test of Jesus' obedience to the Father. During those days, His mind was being shaped, preparing the way for His being the great Teacher one day. Jesus grew mentally, physically, spiritually and socially: "Jesus grew in wisdom and stature, and in favor with God and men" (Luke 2:52).

Sadly, Joseph and Mary forfeited the privilege of seeing how some of these aspects of Jesus' life developed because they wanted to move on. They were miles down the road toward Galilee and would not know what was

43

going on—where it mattered. The real sphere of God's influence and power remained precisely where they had just been!

LEARN TO ACCEPT THE SPIRIT'S SILENCE.

It is equally God's sovereign prerogative sometimes to be *silent*. The question may be asked, "Why didn't Jesus *explain* to His mother that He needed to stay behind in Jerusalem?" I think there is only one answer: He wasn't allowed to do so. There is "a time to be silent" (Eccles. 3:7). It takes faith to stay and even more faith to say nothing.

Obviously God does not tell us all He knows. He doesn't tell us all we'd love to know. In precisely the same way that this rare account of Jesus' life between His birth and public ministry is *all we need to know*—so God tells us only *what* we too *need* to know, and *when* we need to know it.

Jesus was silent regarding the lack of communication to His parents that He must remain behind in Jerusalem. He gives no explanation...no apology. He stayed behind in Jerusalem, but His parents were unaware of it.

Sometimes those who think they should be at the head of the line for receiving a word from the Lord—as if that were their special privilege—are the last to know. Some people with a prophetic gift feel they must maintain their reputation by *always* having a word. Because they have been singularly used in the past they presume they will continue to be on the front line in revealing to their generation what God is going to do next!

If Jesus could withhold communication from His own parents, God can certainly keep silent regarding any of us. I think a lot of "prophetic jealousy" exists among those who have a reputation for being gifted with a word of knowledge or prophecy. You've heard of professional jealousy that exists with doctors and lawyers? Have you also heard of prophetic jealousy? It's worse!

I have little doubt that a rival spirit—not a word from the Lord—is what leads some people to take their stand against what God may be up to in a given time. People who are known for their prophetic gift sometimes put themselves under pressure always to have "a word from the Lord." The people in their ministries expect it. Their followers take it for granted. But if a person other than themselves has a word that doesn't include them—or confirm them—they are often ungracious. "It can't be from God," they say, "or I would know."

God was powerfully at work in Jerusalem. Jesus was at the center of it all. But His own parents—those who knew Him best—weren't in on it. It should be a lesson to you and me. God can use me yesterday, but remain silent today. He can use me today, but speak through someone else tomorrow. He may speak through someone of whom no one has heard. Or he may use someone of whom everybody has heard—but doesn't particularly like. God is sovereign.

This was almost certainly the first time Jesus would be "sitting among the teachers." In ancient times, *sitting* was the posture of authority. A child would be expected to stand in the presence of elders. Luke says Jesus was *sitting*—like a learned rabbi. Most teachers and preachers nowadays stand when they want to be heard. Not the rabbis—they always sat.

Eighteen years later Jesus stood up to read Isaiah 61:1–2. "Then he rolled up the scroll, gave it back to the attendant and *sat down*. The eyes of everyone in the synagogue were fastened on him" (Luke 4:20, emphasis added). Why? He was about to make a daring statement: "Today this scripture is fulfilled in your hearing" (v. 21). He made this statement after He sat down. When He delivered His most famous sermon—the Sermon on the

Mount—He was in His rabbinical posture (Matt. 5:1). He taught one parable after another from the boat in which He "sat" (Matt. 13:2). The fact that His parents found their twelve-year-old son "sitting among the teachers, listening to them and asking them questions" was a preview of things to come (Luke 2:46).

In this practice round of what Jesus would later be doing all the time, Jesus exercised His sovereign prerogative. Years later Jesus would turn His eyes heavenward and say, "I praise you, Father, Lord of heaven and earth, because you have hidden these things from the wise and learned, and revealed them to little children. Yes, Father, for this was your good pleasure" (Matt. 11:25–26). No one knows the Father except the Son—"and those to whom the Son *chooses* to reveal him" (v. 27, emphasis added). "For just as the Father raises the dead and gives them life, even so the Son gives life to whom he is pleased to give it" (John 5:21). The silence of Jesus' noncommunication with His parents—His being silent—spoke volumes. It was a taste of the ministry of the coming Sovereign Redeemer.

WHEN IT'S OVER—IT'S JUST BEGINNING

After the Feast was over, then the best was about to begin. As far as Joseph and Mary were concerned, when the Feast was over—it was over. But as Yogi Berra used to say, "It's not over till it's over." For Jesus' parents, the Feast was it. For Jesus, the Feast was merely the occasion for getting Him where He was. More was about to happen.

Someone has said, "When the meeting is over, the service begins"—meaning that when the meeting at church ends, Christian service in the world begins. I like to phrase it this way: When the church service is over, the meeting begins. The word *meeting* was special in ancient Israel. The Tent of Meeting got its name from

Exodus 33:7: "Now Moses used to take a tent and pitch it outside the camp some distance away, calling it the 'tent of meeting.' Anyone inquiring of the LORD would go to the tent of meeting outside the camp."

The Tent of Meeting was the place where God promised to meet with Moses. And God kept His word, for "the LORD would speak to Moses face to face, as a man speaks with his friend" (Exod. 33:11).

The Feast in Jerusalem was over as far as Joseph and Mary were concerned, but an extraordinary meeting was about to begin—a meeting where Jesus would take center stage. Sometimes a church service before God is finished. But the *meeting*—with God—may suddenly take place even before people leave the building. It may remain for hours.

That is how the Hebrides Revival (1949–1952) is said to have begun. After a service was over, one man was found kneeling at a pew, praying aloud for revival. He kept saying, "Your honor is at stake, Your honor is at stake." God stepped in. Within an hour, hundreds turned up spontaneously at the church. Revival came to the islands and lasted for months.

Any meeting with God often truly begins as we go home and apply what we learned at the church service.

Some people go to church just for the service—the Feast or ceremony—and some go to meet with God. Some go only for the ornateness of the worship; some truly worship by the Spirit of God. Some go to hear the preacher's sermon; some go to hear from God. When I was pastor of my little church in Lower Heyford (a Southern Baptist church near the old Upper Heyford air force base in England), Dr. Lloyd-Jones used to come and preach for me at times. On one occasion an old friend of mine came to hear the doctor preach. That evening, the doctor was at his best. All were enthralled with the

47

power that flowed. God came down. But my dear friend didn't feel a thing. His only comment had to do with Dr. Lloyd-Jones's masterful delivery: "Not one split infinitive or dangling participle." That's all he received.

That day in the temple with Jesus as a young boy, the real meeting was about to begin. But Joseph and Mary were miles down the road, believing Jesus was with them—not in Jerusalem. However, the sphere of the Spirit's action was still in that ancient city. The Feast was but preparation for more to come. What made that particular Feast of the Passover historic was not just remembering what God had done in history—it was witnessing what God was doing then and there. What really mattered was the presence of Jesus in Jerusalem. It was as if the "Tent of Meeting" had returned momentarily.

Some twenty-one years later it would happen again. Had you walked into Jerusalem on Good Friday nearly two thousand years ago and asked, "What is God doing in Jerusalem today?", what do you think the answer would be?

No doubt someone would reply, "Oh, don't you know? It's Passover. We are commemorating what God did in ancient Israel. The only problem is, there is a man dying on a cross just outside the city gate, and we need to make sure he is dead so we can dispose of his body on this holy day." No one—*no one*—at that time would have believed that the person dying on the cross was the pivot point of God's activity. No one knew that "God was reconciling the world to himself in Christ, not counting men's sins against them" (2 Cor. 5:19). The real fulfillment of Passover was literally taking place outside the camp, as it had taken place at the old Tent of Meeting (Exod. 33:7).

The Feast—the ceremony, the church service, the custom or tradition—then is all some ever see. We nullify God's Word by our traditions (Matt. 15:6). The Holy Spirit can completely withdraw, and we wouldn't miss Him, just as Joseph and Mary didn't notice Jesus' absence.

WAIT ON THE SPIRIT

Sometimes the hardest thing in the world to do is to wait. We want the church service to end as quickly as possible so we can get home—where, apparently, our heart is. Joseph and Mary wanted to get home. We do the same. Of course, if the Feast of the Passover was as ceremonial and ritualistic as many of our church services, one cannot blame Jesus' parents for wanting to start the long haul back to Nazareth. I fear that our services are so dull and uninteresting—including the preaching—that people are not motivated to attend church at all. Who can blame them for wanting it all to end as soon as possible?

I have never forgotten something Alex Buchanan said to me: "We must communicate God as well as His Word." That shook me rigid. I always assumed that if I preached the Word—God's Word—that was enough. That, surely, was my calling. Wrong. If the hearers to whom I preach do not experience God *Himself* in the words I speak, I have failed to do my job well. It is possible to preach the Word without the Spirit. Paul said that his gospel came not in word only: "Not simply with words, but also with power" (1 Thess. 1:5). He meant that it is very possible indeed to preach with just words. I fear I have been as guilty as they come at this point. I pray those days are coming to an end as I make my way back to Jerusalem.

Some of us are determined to "make" God speak, even when He is clearly saying nothing. We do it with the Scriptures. We make them say what they are not saying in order to fit them in with our own theological biases.

The old saying, "Where the Scriptures speak, we speak; where the Scriptures are silent, we are silent," is

49

good sense. God doesn't answer the question regarding the origin of evil—why He made the world knowing man would sin and suffer. It is a mystery.

We are not the first to want to unravel the mysteries of God. Moses wanted to unravel the mystery as to how a bush could be on fire and not burn up. So he said to himself, "I will go over and see this strange sight—why the bush does not burn up." But God stepped into the picture:

> When the LORD saw that he had gone over to look, God called to him from within the bush, "Moses! Moses!"
> And Moses said, "Here I am."
> "Do not come any closer," God said. "Take off your sandals, for the place where you are standing is holy ground."
>
> —EXODUS 3:4–5

God's silence is holy ground. While we wait on Him, we must take off our shoes and worship.

Joseph and Mary were not aware of God's silence. They headed toward Galilee, thinking Jesus was with them. Likewise, many of us are unaware of God's silence. We think He is communicating when He isn't. We are on our way, very happy and content, feeling we "do not need a thing" (Rev. 3:17).

We must never be guilty of "making" God speak. Only a charlatan, a soothsayer or a fortuneteller *always* has a word. Sometimes we open the Bible and take the first verse we see as God's word for the moment. God *can* do that—and I can honestly say He has graciously done this with me. But if I am honest, more often than not He tells me *nothing* by this precarious method.

It's an old story. A distraught man decided he would open the Bible as a last-ditch effort to hear from God. His eyes fell upon the words, "And Judas went out and hanged himself." This did not bless him, so he tried it again. His eyes fell on the words, "Go and do likewise." By this time he was nearly at the end of his tether, but he tried one more time. The verse he got was, "What thou doest, do quickly." But that wasn't God speaking at all.

God *was* with Joseph and Mary as they journeyed down the road. But the special presence of Jesus was not with them. Sometimes God lets us move on before the cloud lifts. When that happens, we pay dearly for it. Jonah ran from the Lord and made his bed in the depths—but God was there. (See Jonah 1:3; 2:2; Psalm 139:8.) He pleaded for God's *special* presence to return, and God did (Jon. 2:4; 3:1).

When Joseph and Mary realized their mistake, they headed back to Jerusalem. We all have to do the equivalent of this—go back to where we lost Jesus. But they didn't find Him as easily as they imagined they would. Remember, it is always easier to lose God's special presence than it is to get it back. But there is a way back—but only when we see how presumptuous we have been.

CHAPTER THREE

Finding Out What Pleases the Lord

Find out what pleases the Lord.

—EPHESIANS 5:10

We learn what pleases those closest to us primarily by spending time with them. By trial and error we also discover things they like and dislike. When it is a relationship we really desire to develop, it becomes fun to make the other person happy.

But this is not always easy—even when we have known someone for years. For example, although my wife, Louise, has repeatedly said she doesn't like surprises, I never really believed it because *I* do like surprises. But after countless blunders I came to realize that she really means it! She wants to know the plans I have in mind for birthday or anniversary celebrations *in advance*, and I now adjust to her wishes. She has also had to adjust to many of my eccentricities—like having no heavy discussions late in the evening or in the mornings before two cups of coffee!

The Lord has His own ways, too, and He wants us to know them and adjust to them. We may think they are odd—at first—but the benefits of accepting Him as He is and adjusting to what pleases Him will result in great blessing and peace.

That Paul would urge the Ephesians to "find out" what pleases the Lord can only mean that this was an achievable goal—even without the whole of the New Testament. Presumably the Ephesians had only that one letter from Paul to guide them. (It was hundreds of years before all the church had all of the New Testament as a source.) This means the early church had to find out what pleases the Lord largely by experience—through trial and error. They had to spend time with the Lord and take seriously the warning not to grieve the Holy Spirit (Eph. 4:30).

We have the wonderful advantage of having the whole Bible at our fingertips. This surely leaves us without excuse. And yet if we let the Bible replace the immediate witness, guidance and voice of the Spirit, we quench Him in one stroke. For we too must learn—by experience—what pleases the Lord. This means spending time with the Lord and developing a sensitivity to His ways.

Joseph and Mary knew Jesus better than anybody at the time. No doubt they felt special. After all, they were special. Feeling special can give one a feeling of being a cut above everybody else. It happens to those who have experienced a greater degree of intimacy with God than the average believer has experienced. Unless we are careful, we will not only begin to take ourselves too seriously, but also we will fail to tune into the ways of the Spirit—simply because we already presume that we know them so well.

54

In an earlier chapter, I referred to my own journey to get "back to Jerusalem" and how upset I would sometimes get if I was disturbed during my quiet time. In my efforts to get close to God so that I might not grieve the Spirit so quickly, I would get angry when called to the phone or when my wife or children would interrupt me. Each time that happened I chased the Dove away then and there. My feeling was, "Lord, here I am trying to get closer to You. Why do You allow these things to happen when You know they upset me?" I thought that God would provide some kind of indemnity on my behalf to show His approval of my spending more and more time alone with Him. It became a vicious circle. I prayed more so I wouldn't grieve the Spirit, and would grieve the Spirit in the process. Then I would be upset because I grieved the Spirit! At times, pleasing the Spirit seemed like an impossible task.

This has happened in my time of sermon preparation as well. I need solitude and—above all—peace inside. My own efforts to prepare a sermon are invariably sabotaged if I am upset—all possibility of insight from the Spirit is removed. I would think, *Lord, You have put me where I am. I have to have this sermon ready. What I will say publicly will be recorded and maybe heard around the world. You've got to help me.* God seemed to reply, "Really?"

I have learned that God will not accommodate me by altering His principles just for me. He hems me in and requires me to adjust to the Dove. However justified I may feel at the time for being upset, hurt, resentful or angry, God "stays behind" and lets me carry on—to my embarrassment. I have learned that I must sort things out if I am upset. The key is not God's adjusting to me, but my "going back to Jerusalem." It may require that I apologize—whether to my wife, children, deacons, members, other ministers or friends. It can be most

55

humbling. But it is the only way I can function if I really want the Spirit's anointing.

Since God *could* overrule His own principles and commune with me, even as He did with an angry Jonah, why doesn't He do it? (See Jonah 4:4.) To be honest, He has. He has been so gracious. Otherwise I would never have survived. But I have realized that He has tended to stop communing with me when I step out of His special presence. It seems He has taken my request for a greater anointing seriously! I have been constrained to seek His face all the more, apologize all the more (when necessary), forgive all the more and make the choice simply to be gracious.

WHY MUST WE ADJUST TO THE SPIRIT?

Why won't God bend the rules for us? Why are we put on our own, as it were, to find out what pleases the Lord? God has valid reasons for asking us to adjust to the gentle Holy Spirit. In this chapter I want to suggest some of them.

TO MOLD OUR CHARACTER TO BE MORE LIKE JESUS

Even the Son of God "learned obedience from what he suffered" (Heb. 5:8). I do not know fully all that this means. But in my own experience, being left to myself—where I cannot sense God's conscious presence—is about the most painful thing I can think of. It is said of Hezekiah, "God left him to test him and to know everything that was in his heart" (2 Chron. 32:31).

As far as I can tell, God the Father never hid His face from Jesus except when His Son was on the cross. There Jesus cried out, "My God, my God, why have you forsaken me?" (Matt. 27:46). My conclusion is that in some sense we enter into the sufferings of Jesus—that is, feeling forsaken—whenever God hides His face. If we don't, we should. For when I don't sense His presence, I want to know why. Having to adjust to the Dove forces me to be more like Jesus, painful though it is. I seem to learn no other way.

TO PRODUCE GREATER OBEDIENCE

Obedience is doing what one is told to do. As believers, we get our instructions from the Bible—God's revealed will. We cannot bypass the Bible and opt for a special "word of knowledge" (often a "quick-fix" solution) if we truly want to know God. The more we read the Bible, the more we discover what God wants of us. God wants us to know Him by knowing His Word. Can you say you love God when you don't read His Word and seek His face daily?

The Word of God doesn't adjust to us—we must adjust to it. If you are traveling down an unfamiliar road with a map and get lost, your destination will not suddenly move to where you are. You have to look at the map again, carefully plot your course and adjust to the directions in the map before you will reach your destination. The Bible is like a map; it shows the way to go every day.

We will often get off track in our lives. Sometimes we become angry with God because of the things He allows to happen to us. This can happen when, through a tragedy in the world, we confront the evil that exists in our world. Sometimes we become angry with God because He allows misfortune to enter our personal lives. The only way we will find our way through these detours in our lives is by allowing God, through His Word, to show us the good reason for the things we face. His Word becomes our road map to victory.

We see an example of this in the life of David. David had the noble and God-honoring idea of bringing the ark of the covenant back from its exiled position in the

57

enemy's land to Jerusalem. But David's attempt to make this happen was a failure. The only thanks David seemed to get from God was that Uzzah was struck dead merely because he tried to steady the ark with his hand when he thought it might topple over. The ark had been set on a cart that was pulled along by oxen. It was to travel a mere distance of approximately twenty miles.

> When they came to the threshing floor of Nacon, Uzzah reached out and took hold of the ark of God, because the oxen stumbled. The Lord's anger burned against Uzzah because of his irreverent act; therefore God struck him down and he died there beside the ark of God.
>
> —2 SAMUEL 6:6–7

This made David angry. One can understand why. All David was trying to do was to restore the glory of God in Jerusalem! Would God be pleased? Certainly. But God wouldn't bend the rules for David, no matter how lofty or honoring to God David's idea was. After a while, David cooled off and sought the Lord. Upon closer reflection he discovered he hadn't obeyed God's plain word on the matter: "We didn't enquire of him about how to do it in the prescribed way," he admitted (1 Chron. 15:13). God had instructed that only priests could carry the ark.

In order to get back on track with God, David had to make the adjustment to God's ways. He had to take the ark off that cart and carry it the way God's Word prescribed. Eventually he moved the ark to Jerusalem, and all ended well (2 Sam. 6:14–19).

It's very important to remember that there *was* a reason things didn't work out at first.

Another example of our need to adjust to the Spirit can be seen in the story of Jesus staying behind in the Judean desert rather than going to heal Lazarus as soon as the report came that Lazarus was ill. (See John 11.) Jesus could have made it to Lazarus in time to heal him and prevent his dying. But He waited—then showed up four days after the funeral! Mary and Martha each said, "Lord, if you had been here, my brother would not have died" (John 11:21, 32).

In other words, it made no sense that Jesus didn't turn up. But at the end of the day, it was evident that Jesus had a good reason for delaying after all. Jesus thought that raising Lazarus from the dead was a better idea than keeping him from dying. This simply shows how things that we don't understand at first can be understood later—if we will wait.

TO SHOW HOW MUCH WE REALLY DO LOVE GOD

We prove our love for God partly by our reaction to the knowledge that we grieved the Spirit. Our first reaction, like David's, may be anger. When we first discover that we have grieved the Spirit, it is often much like David's not understanding how an apparently innocent thing like Uzzah's touching the ark could warrant such wrath from God. But, like David, we must mellow and think again. There is always a reason for the Dove's fluttering away. Our love for God is shown by turning to Him *again* and inquiring of Him as David did. "One thing I ask of the LORD, this is what I seek: that I may dwell in the house of the LORD all the days of my life, to gaze upon the beauty of the LORD and to seek him in his temple" (Ps. 27:4).

It is a wonderful thing to realize that we really do love God, especially when we are so conscious of our unworthiness and inadequacies. It is at those times that God lets us know He is aware that we really do love Him. But what if God doesn't let us feel this way? In the absence of that assurance, we must show we love God—not by

59

persistent resentment that grieves the Spirit so easily, but by persevering in seeking His face *all the more*.

> So do not throw away your confidence; it will be richly rewarded. You need to persevere so that when you have done the will of God, you will receive what He has promised. For in just a very little while,
>
> "He who is coming will come and will not delay.
> But my righteous one will live by faith.
> And if he shrinks back,
> I will not be pleased with him."
>
> —HEBREWS 10:35–38

> However, as it is written: "No eye has seen, no ear has heard, no mind has conceived what God has prepared for those who love him."
>
> —1 CORINTHIANS 2:9

TO DEVELOP A SENSE OF SIN

There was a time in my life when this thought was alien to me. That is, until I was baptized by the Holy Spirit. Then 1 John 1:8 became real to me: "If we claim to be without sin, we deceive ourselves and the truth is not in us." Sadly, there was a time when I thought, *I have no sin*. But that was largely because of a faulty theology and because I excused any sin as a mistake, error or "shortcoming." I dared not use the word *sin*.

But that changed. Not that I began sinning to prove I was a sinner, but because the greater sense of *God* resulted in a greater sense of sin. It happened to Isaiah when he saw the glory of God: "'Woe to me!' I cried. 'I am ruined! For I am a man of unclean lips, and I live among a people of unclean lips, and my eyes have seen the King, the LORD Almighty'" (Isa. 6:5).

When we discover what grieves the Holy Spirit we learn more deeply what sin is. It has far more to do with what we are like within ourselves than it has to do with things some Christians have called *sin*—kinds of entertainment, dress and what is commonly called "worldliness" in some circles. I am not suggesting that we approve of such sin. But *not doing* some things can camouflage as godliness and give a self-righteous feeling.

I've known people who condemn movie-attending and trendy styles who think nothing of having an out-and-out fight with another person in the church's parking lot—and feel no conviction of sin for it at all! Adjusting to the Dove means developing a sensitivity *to* Him by coming to terms with what hurts His feelings. In such a way we develop a true sense of sin.

TO LET US SEE BY EXPERIENCE THE VERY THINGS THAT GRIEVE THE HOLY SPIRIT

The things that grieve the Spirit are listed in Ephesians 4:30–5:7:

> And do not grieve the Holy Spirit of God, with whom you were sealed for the day of redemption. Get rid of all bitterness, rage and anger, brawling and slander, along with every form of malice. Be kind and compassionate to one another, forgiving each other, just as in Christ God forgave you.
>
> Be imitators of God, therefore, as dearly loved children and live a life of love, just as Christ loved us and gave himself up for us as a fragrant offering and sacrifice to God.
>
> But among you there must not be even a hint of sexual immorality, or of any kind of impurity, or of greed, because these are improper for God's holy people. Nor should there be obscenity, foolish talk or coarse joking, which are out of place, but rather thanksgiving. For of this you can be sure: No immoral, impure or greedy person—such a man is an idolater—has any inheritance in

the kingdom of Christ and of God. Let no one deceive you with empty words, for because of such things God's wrath comes on those who are disobedient. Therefore do not be partners with them.

Sometimes when we read these verses they tend to slip past us like water falling off a duck's back. Certainly we agree that these warnings are valid. But so many times we give assent in our heads—yet our hearts do not respond with improved behavior. My friend Robert Amess says that the longest journey is from "the head to the heart." It isn't until the knowledge lodges in the heart that our outlook changes.

Many times it isn't until we realize the Dove has quietly flown away that we become aware of the truth in these verses from Ephesians. They are packed with importance, and we often have to discover through trial and error the things that chase the Dove away. The things mentioned in these verses seem small at first. But eventually they become very important, and learning to avoid displeasing the Dove becomes incorporated into a lifestyle that tends not to grieve the Spirit so often. After all, the Dove *remained* on Jesus. Therefore, our goal should be to have the Dove remain on us for as long as possible—allowing His ungrieved presence to stay with us consistently. In any case, one day God will take us all home where "we shall be like him, for we shall see him as he is" (1 John 3:2). Learning how not to grieve the Spirit prepares us for that glorious moment.

To experience as soon as possible that
the Spirit is grieved

As I have emphasized from the outset of this book, the Spirit tends to withdraw in such a manner that we feel nothing at all. But there is an exception to this. One of my chief aims in writing this book is precisely this: I want to feel it inside the moment He is grieved—and I want that for you, too. If we develop such a sensitivity to His presence, we will sense it instantly when He is disturbed. And we will sense instantly when He is pleased.

When He is disturbed I begin to lose peace. It may happen when I am in conversation with someone. It may happen when I am answering a letter. An uneasiness inside emerges, a gentle signal that I am either saying something, listening to something or about to agree to something that is not pleasing to the Lord. When this occurs there is only one thing to do: Stop. I may ask that we change the subject (in an unobtrusive manner)—I may simply rewrite what I just said. By following this "check" from the Spirit (that's probably the best word for it), I prevent myself from losing communion with the Lord. In addition, I don't have to deal with regret for other things down the road. What is quite extraordinary (although we shouldn't be so surprised) is that with following this "check" (a negative feeling) comes a wonderful peace.

But there is also a positive side to this issue. I can have an overwhelming peace from the knowledge that the Spirit approves of me. It is like a green light that sets me free to proceed in the manner I have been thinking. By this I know I am safe.

The recognition of this peace—and the green light I feel to proceed—enables me to avoid falling into the traps of sin we read about in Ephesians 4:30–5:7. By obeying the inner testimony of the Spirit I avoid the outer trap of sin. That is the way Christians lived before they had the complete Bible. And that is the way we should live today, now that we have His complete Word!

To teach us graciousness

Paul said, "Let your gentleness ["moderation"—KJV] be evident to all" (Phil. 4:5). This word comes from a Greek word that meant (in the ancient Hellenistic world) "not to throw the book at someone, but let him or her off the hook." It comes down to our English word *graciousness*.

Being gracious is a choice. We can choose to throw the book at someone—or to be gracious. It is a grace that doesn't come naturally or easily. But doing it is being like Jesus. It is the way God is to us. We show our gratitude to God for His graciousness by being gracious.

TO SHOW THAT WE REALLY DO WANT A GREATER ANOINTING

I am grateful to Dottie Oates, a friend of ours, who asked, "Is it selfish to want to be filled more and more with the Holy Spirit?" She had asked that I pray for her in this manner. Then she began to feel guilty that this was her uttermost desire!

The truth is, the very desire for a greater anointing is supernatural. It is possible that a few years before Dottie would not have even thought of such a request! But as Jackie Pullinger once said to me, "To the spiritual person the supernatural seems natural." So it is not *selfish*; it is *supernatural*. But to the one who wants a greater anointing *so much*, it may seem selfish!

How can we demonstrate our great desire for a greater anointing? It is not necessarily demonstrated by how often we go forward for prayer ministry at church or by how much we pray in private. The proof of wanting a greater anointing is that we *grieve when we grieve the Spirit* and, consequently, adjust to Him.

If you have told God you want a greater anointing more than anything in the world, I can safely promise you that He will give you dozens of tests almost daily to prove that you really do mean what you have said!

Adjusting to the Dove is not easy. It is inconvenient. It requires making major changes in some of the habits that have never bothered us before. The question is: How far are you and I prepared to go in developing an acute sensitivity to the Holy Spirit's ways? I pray it will not be said of us, "They have not known my ways," as God said of ancient Israel. By not knowing His way, Israel forfeited her inheritance (Ps. 95:10).

Adjusting to the Dove is welcoming His presence. It is also giving Him no cause to leave.

How do we welcome Him? For one thing, tell Him! Have you often addressed the Holy Spirit with these words, "Holy Spirit, I welcome You"? Do this. Tell Him He is most welcome. Doing this is, in my opinion, virtually the first thing we must utter to God—together with the prayer for the sprinkling of Christ's blood on us—every single morning of our lives.

You may say, "He already knows He is welcome." Really? Do you not think He would love to hear you tell Him this? When you visit someone, and that person says to you, "You are most welcome here," doesn't it make you feel good?

Is the Holy Spirit so sensitive that He needs to be told He is welcome? Perhaps. Most people, sadly, want little or nothing to do with Him. You can prove you are different by welcoming Him! You can develop a deeper intimacy with the Lord by talking to Him about the most obvious and simple things—just as you would do with a friend.

But welcome Him to come in the manner He chooses. He may test your willingness in several ways. He may gently suggest that your attitude toward someone is not right. If you push this thought to one side, the chances are that the Spirit may well unobtrusively slip away. You cannot be selective in the manner He may choose to come. When the Spirit departs like this, as I have been saying, you usually feel nothing at first. And yet you *do* feel something—righteous in yourself that your attitude is justified. You might even feel that God Himself is saying, "Well done. You are right to feel hurt." But that is *not* the Holy Spirit.

I've been in that position a thousand times. I know what it is to feel so upset that *they* could do such a thing! Often I have conversations with myself, imagining what I will say to one person, what I will tell another. I intend to set the record straight. I rehearse what the other person did. "That can't be right," I keep saying. I even imagine that I hear God saying, "Of course that's not right." I start to feel good, as if God is on *my* side—*not theirs*. I tell myself that I sense the presence of the heavenly Dove. Wrong! If anything, it's a pigeon. We will learn more of this in chapter eight.

When I welcome the Holy Spirit I must take Him as He wants to come. He may flood my soul with joy and peace. That is almost always my first preference. He may highlight a verse as I read the Bible, showing me something I hadn't seen before. That too is near the top of what I hope He will do. I love it when He applies the Word to a current situation in such a manner that I *know* what to do that day. I don't like it, however, when that Word instructs me to apologize to my wife—or a deacon, friend or fellow minister—before I can feel great peace again.

Of one thing we can be sure, however. The *end result* of the Holy Spirit's manifestation provides considerable inner peace. Peace. It is wonderful and worth all the pain of having to move outside our comfort zone.

HOW TO AVOID THE SPIRIT'S DEPARTURE

Adjusting to the Spirit, then, is welcoming His presence while giving Him no cause to leave. What are the things we need to do to prevent the Dove from flying quietly away? I want to share several things that I've learned as a result of my search to "find out what pleases the Lord."

Most of these principles relate to times when we are tempted to panic or get upset.

LETTING THINGS BE

Don't try to straighten out negative and unpleasant things—let God do it His way and in His time. We begin this with an inward attitude—a deliberate and conscious choice. For me, I must make a conscious choice not to immediately roll up my sleeves, step in and "fight fire with fire"—or to criticize. My temperament always tugs me in that direction. For me, letting things be means *tongue control.* Maybe you are like me in this regard. If you are, as I have found out…it ain't easy!

> Likewise the tongue is a small part of the body, but it makes great boasts. Consider what a great forest is set on fire by a small spark. The tongue also is a fire, a world of evil among the parts of the body. It corrupts the whole person, sets the whole course of his life on fire, and is itself set on fire by hell.
>
> —JAMES 3:5–6

67

The spark that can set a forest on fire is always present. What I say when I am confronted with negative, unpleasant circumstances—and how I say it—can determine if the Dove stays put or quietly flies away. I want the Spirit to stay. But the temptation to drive Him away by my words or actions can be terrific, sometimes (so it often seems at first) a temptation too great! But no. "No temptation has seized you except what is common to man. And God is faithful; he will not let you be tempted beyond what you can bear. But when you are tempted, he will also provide a way out so that you can stand up under it" (1 Cor. 10:13). The "way out" is, in this case, *letting things be.*

Letting things be may be only a test to see whether I truly want the Dove to remain. By doing this I continue to allow God to be in control—which is the best way to live. God has given many promises to the one who can harness his own tongue to trust God to be in control: "You will keep in perfect peace him whose mind is steadfast, because he trusts in you" (Isa. 26:3). "In quietness and trust is your strength" (Isa. 30:15). "When words are many, sin is not absent, but he who holds his tongue is wise" (Prov. 10:19).

It is one thing to believe in the sovereignty of God in principle, quite another to do so in practice. The proof of my confidence in God's sovereignty in the matter of practice is that I do nothing. No panic. I just leave it alone and say nothing.

OVERLOOKING OFFENSE

Overlooking unpacks the principle and practice of letting things be. Overlooking offense is the challenge of challenges when you are faced with an accusation (true or false), insult or any form of unfairness. It takes the principle and practice of letting things be one step further: "A man's wisdom gives him patience; it is to his glory to overlook an offense" (Prov. 19:11). One definition of *overlooking* is "to take no notice of, to allow an offense to go unpunished."

This is graciousness. You act (sincerely) as though you didn't notice. I am not referring to social injustice in these pages, or to things like *refusing to be involved* when you see a crime. I am only referring to one's inner reaction to being verbally abused. Of course you defend yourself when you are physically attacked—you also step in (if possible) when you see it happening to another. These actions would not grieve the Spirit; rather, if anything, you would be accessing the Holy Spirit's power by such a response.

The type of graciousness to which I refer is when you

choose to overlook and exercise your own verbal self-control when you are maligned personally by a friend or enemy, a boss or a spouse. In Proverbs 25:2 we read, "It is the glory of God to conceal a matter." This is what God has done for us by His Son's death on the cross. Our sins are concealed. "As far as the east is from the west, so far has he removed our transgressions from us" (Ps. 103:12). For this reason we forgive "just as in Christ God forgave you" (Eph. 4:32). It is what Jesus Himself did (Luke 23:34). We conceal what could be told and brought out into the open. In this way we insure the Dove's presence. It explains how the Dove remained on Jesus right to the end.

BECOMING VULNERABLE

Being vulnerable is not cowardice or being a "wimp." In fact, it is the opposite—it is being a tower of strength. It is what Paul means by becoming a *man* (1 Cor. 13:11). It is when you are so strong inside that you do not take yourself so seriously. *Vulnerability* means the ability to be hurt, being unprotected. Our friend Alan Bell says that love is "moving forward without protecting yourself." Becoming vulnerable is therefore the opposite of the sin of self-protection.

Jesus was the strongest man who ever lived. He had the power to stop the entire crucifixion proceedings. He proved that by manifesting only a degree of His power when the chief priests and soldiers came to arrest Him. The Word tells us that when the soldiers surrounded Him in the garden, suddenly dozens (some scholars think it was hundreds) all "fell to the ground" (John 18:6). But Jesus *chose* to be vulnerable. Paul said that Jesus was "crucified in weakness," a chosen vulnerability (2 Cor. 13:4).

Many marriages on the rocks could be healed overnight if both husband and wife would become vulnerable,

69

stop protecting himself or herself and stop pointing the finger. I believe tension in marriages is one of the chief causes for the Holy Spirit to be grieved today.

Taking myself too seriously grieves the Spirit and robs me of anointing. King Saul's taking himself too seriously led to his becoming yesterday's man. (See 1 Samuel 13:9–14; 16:1.) The issue of "who gets the credit" paralyzes many ministers today—so many want to be noticed and given due recognition. But when you see such a response it is certain that the Dove is no longer anywhere close.

I am reminded of a small plaque that former President Ronald Reagan kept on his desk. It read: "There is no limit to how far a person can go as long as he doesn't care who gets the credit." Many a person forfeits greater usefulness because he or she can't bear the thought of not getting deserved credit for something. Neither can many people tolerate someone else's getting credit for something they did themselves. I can understand this. But it is a wonderful inner release—and glorifying to God—to be utterly self-effacing and to abandon the praise of people. God can trust such a person with a wider ministry.

SETTING PEOPLE FREE

The ministry of emancipation is what Jesus and the Holy Spirit are all about. The problem is, we want to control things. I doubt there is a much greater sin than deliberately leaving a person in the bondage of guilt when it lies within our power to emancipate that person.

Emancipating another person requires several steps. We must:

- Forgive that person totally by refusing to tell what we know.

- Keep the person from feeling intimidated.

    ல Enable the person to forgive himself or herself.

    ல Let the person save face.

If you want to make a friend forever, let that person *save face*. Allow another a sense of self-esteem, a sense of dignity and self-worth. When Prime Minister Joseph of Egypt looked at his eleven scared brothers and said, "It was not you who sent me here, but God," he was letting each of them save face (Gen. 45:8). They had tried to destroy him twenty-two years before, and their guilt was unthinkably deep. Joseph knew that. He set them free. "God intended it for good," he told them (Gen. 50:20). How that must have felt!

We can control people not only by guilt, but also by keeping them under our thumb in order to manipulate them. The Holy Spirit does not manipulate us—He sets us free. Many strong leaders (owing largely to their own insecurity) keep their followers under control by making them feel disloyal if they do not dot every *i* and cross every *t* as *they* would do. Such leaders, I believe, are in danger of quenching the Holy Spirit and robbing people of freedom. The Holy Spirit is in the business of emancipating, and when we enjoy His ungrieved and unquenched presence, we will *keep* it by giving up personal control of people.

God has done that with each of us. He set us free from our past. He promises that all things work together for *good* to those who love Him, who are called according to His purpose (Rom. 8:28, KJV). We have the high privilege of *being Jesus to others*—setting them free. The Holy Spirit loves this response from us. The Dove is perfectly at home with those who let other people save face.

At first we may wish that God would bend the principles of the Holy Spirit for us. But at the end of the day we will

71

thank God, who is no respecter of persons, for His patience with us. Most of all we will be grateful that we have experienced our own ability to adjust to the Dove—namely, to find out for ourselves what pleases God.

CHAPTER FOUR

Why Is God Sometimes Silent?

Truly you are a God who hides himself, O God and
Savior of Israel.

—Isaiah 45:15

Oswald Chambers once asked a provoking question:
"Am I close enough to God to feel secure when He
is silent?" In other words, must I have a constant
two-way communication with God to feel approved and
loved by Him? Paul exhorted Timothy to "be instant in
season, out of season" (2 Tim. 4:2, KJV). We must develop
a maturity that does not panic "between the times"—to
use a helpful phrase from Richard Bewes. *In season* is a
time of refreshing when God clearly manifests Himself.
Out of season is when He seems to hide His face from us,
those times when He is silent.

God wants us to learn as much from His silence as
we learn from His absence. For example, often we learn

more about ourselves when God hides Himself than in times of conscious blessing. His silence is like taking an examination in which we must demonstrate how much we have learned about His "ways."

Jesus was silent to His parents about His plans to stay behind to talk with the temple leaders as a young boy. Probably His reason for not telling them had something to do with the nature of what He was about to learn, and share, with the teachers in the temple courts. He truly was about His *Father's* business—something greater than His earthly responsibilities to His parents. But there was far more than that in the divine strategy—it was also a learning experience for Joseph and Mary. It was their first "practice round." They had a lot to learn.

It is very likely that they weren't prepared for the day they would have to relinquish Jesus to the purpose for which He had been sent to them. Even before His birth they had been told of His coming—and of His purpose for coming. How could they ever forget the miraculous nature and circumstances of His birth? The angel Gabriel had been sent to Mary when she was a virgin:

> "You will be with child and give birth to a son, and you are to give him the name Jesus. He will be great and will be called the Son of the Most High. The Lord God will give him the throne of his father David, and he will reign over the house of Jacob forever; his kingdom will never end."
>
> "How will this be," Mary asked the angel, "since I am a virgin?"
>
> The angel answered, "The Holy Spirit will come upon you, and the power of the Most High will overshadow you. So the holy one to be born will be called the Son of God."
>
> —LUKE 1:31–35

Joseph also had been given a prophetic word in a dream:

> Joseph son of David, do not be afraid to take Mary
> home as your wife, because what is conceived in her is
> from the Holy Spirit. She will give birth to a son, and you
> are to give him the name Jesus, because he will save his
> people from their sins.
>
> —MATTHEW 1:20–21

They may have remembered these events nearly every time they looked at Jesus. They must have known that one day everything would change and they would have to let Him go, releasing Him to the Father who sent Him. But knowing that day *would come* and knowing that day *had come* were two different things. *Surely it's a long way off,* they may have thought. And indeed, it was still a good while before He finally left home for good.

So Jesus' Bar Mitzvah turned out to be a traumatic event for Joseph and Mary. It would be their first taste of what it would be like when He struck out on His own.

Was it necessary that this memorable event take place—as if only for their sakes? Yes. Although Jesus was obedient to them once they headed for Nazareth (Luke 2:51), I suspect that from then on they felt a certain detachment regarding Him. Perhaps it kept them from being too controlling. They had been put in their place—and Jesus had demonstrated His place.

This needs to happen to all of us. Once we get a taste of intimacy with God, we need a taste of His apparent aloofness as well. If that doesn't happen, almost always we begin to take ourselves too seriously. We imagine ourselves to be closer to God than we really are and think we know more about Him than we actually do.

An intimate, unique experience of some kind with God is important for each of us to have. It can be the best thing that can happen to us—but it can also be

75

dangerous. After such an experience we can express a spiritual arrogance and pride that exalts us, in our own eyes, above other "less special" believers. If that happens, perhaps the only thing that can bring us back to a humble awareness of our spiritual position is for God Himself to desert us momentarily. Spiritual pride is the most obnoxious kind of pride. To claim to have a unique "hot line" to God is, first of all, *not* something that God ever gives to us unconditionally. It would destroy us. It would make us smug, pompous and unteachable.

People who suppose they have this sort of relationship with God lack in both teachability and accountability. They sometimes think they are spiritually superior to all who try to help them. The only thing that will possibly help them is for God Himself to "stay behind" while they carry on in their presumption.

It happened to me as I described above. It hurt very much, and I couldn't understand it for a while. God appeared to betray me. He seemed to be like an enemy, as though He didn't know me. His manner of communicating and showing up stopped. Not that I noticed it at first. The momentum and memory of a sustained intimacy over a good while camouflaged as His real presence until I came to terms with His absence.

It happens, I believe, to nearly every person who has had an authentic experience with the Holy Spirit. God hides His face—suddenly and without notice. No apology. Just silence. The explanation comes (usually) much, much later.

WHY GOD STAYS BEHIND

Why does God do this? Why does He "stay behind"?

TO SHOW WHAT IS IN OUR HEARTS

Moses warned the Israelites, "Remember how the LORD your God led you all the way in the desert these forty years, to humble you and to test you in order to know what was in your heart, whether or not you would keep his commands" (Deut. 8:2). When we are on the receiving end of an unusual manifestation of God, we tend to feel so sure we will always be obedient. Peter thought it. "Even if all fall away on account of you, I never will" (Matt. 26:33). He was so wrong. He thought he was better than all the rest.

Moses needed to experience the "betrayal barrier"—a feeling that God has turned against you. Moses wasn't prepared for what immediately followed once he made the heroic decision to leave the palace of Pharaoh "rather than to enjoy the pleasures of sin" (Heb. 11:25). Perhaps he thought that God would send a thousand angels to congratulate him. I only know he jumped the gun by anticipating an instant success and acceptance among his people, the Hebrews. He thought he had endeared himself to them by killing an Egyptian. Wrong. "Moses thought that his own people would realize that God was using him to rescue them, but they did not" (Acts 7:25). He had to wait another forty years before he was ready to be used. As Dr. Lloyd-Jones once said to me, "The worst thing that can happen to a man is to succeed before he is ready."

Hezekiah was one of Israel's greatest kings. He had seen God step into his life in an extraordinary manner again and again.

> Hezekiah trusted in the LORD, the God of Israel. There was no one like him among all the kings of Judah, either before him or after him. He held fast to the LORD and did not cease to follow him; he kept the commands the LORD had given Moses. And the LORD was with him; he was successful in whatever he undertook.
>
> —2 KINGS 18:5–7

But that is not the whole story. His heart later became

proud (2 Chron. 32:25). As a result, "God left him to test him and to know everything that was in his heart" (2 Chron. 32:31). It is one thing for the manifestation of God's glory to test us through a powerful supernatural experience. As we saw earlier, God did that with Isaiah, and he responded, "Woe is me!" (See Isaiah 6:1–5.) Yet it is another thing for God to make us aware of what we are like by seeming to desert us—by staying behind. But often He must do this because we are shut up to seeing ourselves as we really are. Would that we could, for it is not a pretty sight: "The heart is deceitful above all things and beyond cure. Who can understand it?" (Jer. 17:9).

TO GIVE US OBJECTIVITY ABOUT OURSELVES

This is stating the previous point in a slightly different way. To have objectivity about ourselves is to rise above our feelings and prejudices. It is to see ourselves as we truly are—not where we have assumed we are. Or, as Robert Burns put it:

> O wad sum powr the giftie gie us,
> To see oursels as ithers see us![1]

God does us an enormous favor by giving us a glimpse of ourselves through other people's eyes. It is a sobering experience. And if God does not do this for us by an immediate operation of the Spirit, He may use another to come alongside and tell us the truth. A true friend will do this. I have one or two friends who have the guts to talk to me like this. Sometimes the truth comes from our enemies. The latter may not have the best intentions, but if the truth of their words can be taken on board, we are all the better for it. A true friend, however, is someone who knows all about you and still likes you—and will gently and lovingly slip in a word we need to hear.

At times, it is the Lord's presence in our lives that results in an awareness of sin—as in Isaiah's experience

(Isa. 6:1–6). But it does not follow that His presence *always* does that. Indeed, it is His withdrawal from us instead that may bring that awareness. It is so easy to take His presence for granted, as Joseph and Mary obviously did.

One of the most painful lessons I have learned was during my first year at Trevecca Nazarene College. I was eighteen and enrolled in a course called "Introduction to the New Testament." Toward the end of the term the professor said, "Next week we get to the Book of Revelation—which I don't understand, but I will try to introduce it. I don't suppose there is anybody here who understands this book, is there?"

Yes, there was—me. I raised my hand without the slightest blush on my countenance. "Oh, Mr. Kendall, do you understand the Book of Revelation?" the professor asked.

"I do," I said with a straight face. And why shouldn't I? I had read a book on it. Moreover, my pastor, Dr. L. B. Hicks, had his charts (in Technicolor) that stretched a mile wide and several yards high. He lectured on Revelation every Wednesday night. I felt sorry for the deprived professor.

Then he said to me, "Would you like to teach the lesson next week, Mr. Kendall?" My time had at last come. I knew I was sent to Trevecca for such a time as this! I accepted the offer.

The day came. I lectured on the Book of Revelation. I told all I knew. It went on for fifty minutes. The bell rang, the students got up—they were amazingly able to do so—and filed out. I was surprised that they were not in awe, and that they seemed just a little bit glad to leave. I had expected them all to line up and fawn all over me—with not a little reverence as well. No. They all left the room. However, there was one fellow student who came up to me. I thought to myself, *It's about time*. He asked,

"Do you always hold your head to one side and talk with your jaw going back and forth?"

I was humiliated. The dear professor kindly stayed behind. He thanked me. "But what do you think?" I asked.

"I've heard all that before," he said. "Who knows, you may be right." I was put in my place. I still haven't fully recovered, neither would I boast today that I perfectly understand the Book of Revelation! But there was a positive fallout from the experience—I was given a measure of objectivity about myself. The Lord stayed behind as I carried on with pompous naiveté. It was the best thing that could have happened to me.

My painful experience in trying to show off at Trevecca is somewhat matched by a similar story concerning a famous preacher. As a young man he preached his first sermon in a country church in Tennessee. No one said a word. As the young preacher was driven home, nobody in the car was saying a thing. But finally one of the men in the car—a farmer—broke the silence, knowing the young man hoped for a little bit of feedback. "Well, young man, I'll tell you: You went down the deepest and stayed down the longest and, I really do believe, brought up the least of anybody I've ever heard." Now that was a bit cruel. But as my old friend Reverend C. B. Fugett used to say to me, "Every compliment, every bouquet, every pat on the back I ever received did perhaps a *little* more to make me a better person. But every jolt, every kick and every criticism always ended up doing me a *world of good.*"

The Lord stays behind by letting the people we know be people, and the result, if we listen without being defensive, will bring us to greater objectivity about ourselves.

It is not always by negative input that we come to a great objectivity about ourselves. In 1970, my church in Fort Lauderdale allowed me to attend a course in California led by Dr. Clyde Narramore. It was the first time I sat in on a twenty-hour counseling session with a dozen others. The upshot of this for me was that I saw myself in a way I had not remotely considered. It was sobering, but it also encouraged me to see some positive aspects of my personality, which gave me a measure of confidence.

TO SEE WHAT OUR REACTION WILL BE

Will we carry on, thinking God is with us, or will we notice His absence at once? Joseph and Mary did not miss His presence because they thought He *was* present. As far as we know, Jesus had never done anything like that before, so why should they think He was not there?

As long as the Lord is *consciously* with us, there usually isn't much of a test to our faith. But there is a memorable first time when God hides His face. Hezekiah experienced it, as we saw earlier: "God left him to test him and to know everything that was in his heart" (2 Chron. 32:31). This experience may be abrupt—sudden, so that it is immediately noticeable. It may be accompanied by an acute sense of loss. It may come by discovering that you were wrong about an opinion you held or advice you gave another. You may have thought God gave you a definite word, only to discover later that it could not really have come from God after all. But however this experience comes—it will be felt.

> How tedious and tasteless the hours,
> When Jesus no longer I see!
> Sweet prospects, sweet birds and sweet flow'rs,
> Have lost all their sweetness to me;
> The midsummer sun shines but dim,
> The fields strive in vain to look gay;
> But when I am happy in Him,
> December's as pleasant as May.[2]

There comes a time when, after being "tutored" by the

81

Lord, He steps back and sees how we do, as it were, on our own. My parents tell me that I began to walk when I was about ten months old. They taught me to walk by pinning a diaper around my waist. They held on to the diaper and walked beside me, but eventually they stayed behind as I walked on. When I discovered they were no longer next to me, I fell down and cried. Yet I had shown that I could walk. The diaper around my waist made me feel that I had them with me as well. Sometimes we all do that—we feel something that tells us Jesus is there, when, in fact, we are tied to our comfort zone.

A well-known story comes out of Charles G. Finney's era. On one occasion he kept a great crowd waiting. Several hymns were sung, but Finney did not arrive. Those who were in charge of the meeting knew that he was on the premises. But when it came time for him to be introduced, he had not appeared. A man was sent back to the vestry, where he heard Finney's voice trembling from behind a closed door. Finney was saying, "I won't go out there unless You go with me."

The man brought this report back to the restless congregation. Now they gladly waited. It was worth waiting for. When Finney finally appeared, a great anointing settled on the congregation. Without his uttering a word, scores of people rushed to the front and fell on their knees to pray and confess their sins.

Finney's experience was much like one that Moses experienced. In the midst of leading the Israelites to the Promised Land, Moses needed assurance that God was with them. In Exodus 33:15, Moses said, "If your Presence does not go with us, do not send us up from here."

I have a sermon based on Hebrews 4:16 that I have preached countless times. Nearly every preacher has his "sugar stick," and that one is probably mine. In January 1996 I was invited by John Arnott to preach at the Airport

Christian Fellowship in Toronto on the second anniversary of the "Toronto Blessing."[3] I couldn't decide what to preach. The truth is, God gave me nothing.

But when I was introduced, I resorted to my sugar stick. I read Hebrews 4:14–16 with great difficulty. I had never had this problem before. But when I started to preach, I couldn't make sense of a single sentence. The congregation loved every minute of it. There was my wife, Louise, sitting right behind John and Carol Arnott—laughing uncontrollably. Next to her was Lyndon Bowring, doing just the same. I tried to ignore them. For the second and third times I started: "The Epistle to the Hebrews was written to discouraged Christians." By now the crowd was really beginning to take off. They could see what was happening to me, and I was not enjoying it one bit. I was completely unable to proceed. It was like a nightmare, and yet I hoped it was. I was praying like mad. God seemed a million miles away to me.

"God, help me," I uttered with all my heart and strength. I tried a fourth time: "This verse answers a lot of questions." The crowd was now laughing with such volume that all I could think of was this word—or rather, lack of it—reaching across the Atlantic and giving ammunition to all my critics who felt I was abandoning my expository preaching ministry for the sake of the Toronto Blessing. I knew that if I failed to preach that night—and fell flat on the floor (my worst fear) in front of four thousand people and several video cameras—I would play right into the hands of all who were waiting to say, "I told you so." I tried a fifth time: "A sentence that asks a question is called an interrogatory sentence." By now the crowd could see God at work as I tried helplessly to carry on.

God at work? Yes. I have never experienced anything like it in my life. Had someone offered me one million dollars in cash—tax free—to preach that sermon I had

83

preached over fifty times, I could not have done it. I have never been drunk—unless it was on this occasion. But I tried again: "This verse answers a lot of questions: Who? How? What..." I could say no more. I called on all the brainpower and energy at my disposal. But to no avail.

The Lord had stayed behind! In this case, I could not preach that sermon at all. After fifteen minutes, mercifully a word came into my head: Hebrews 13:13. Quickly I turned to see what that verse said. It read: "Let us, then, go to him outside the camp, bearing the disgrace he bore."

Suddenly I had presence of mind and began my sermon. In seconds the laughter subsided. You could almost hear a pin drop. Without any notes or preparation I preached on the need to go outside the camp, bearing the reproach of Jesus. Half an hour later, more than two hundred people, including many ministers, came forward when I gave an appeal. I continue to run into people who tell me their lives were changed that night.

84

I do not know why God didn't give me Hebrews 13:13 as a text before I went up to the platform. I didn't know it at the time—I learned it later—but *that was the first day* the name of the church had been changed from Airport Vineyard Fellowship to Airport Christian Fellowship. That church had just been disenfranchised, and they were now outside the camp. Without my knowledge, God had prepared a word for them—through that text—and He had to get my attention so He could use me to deliver it!

TO SEE IF WE CAN ACT UPON THE THINGS WE HAVE LEARNED IN HIS PRESENCE ONCE WE ARE "ON OUR OWN"

If we collapse the moment the Lord withdraws His special presence, it suggests we haven't learned much. Whereas we dare not proceed without Him, sometimes we have no choice but to get on with our calling and make the most of the situation. I doubt that the Lord expects me to wait in the vestry as Charles Finney did every Sunday morning. I fear that if I did, I might never go out at all.

The late Bishop Festo Kivenge told of an argument he and his wife had just before he was scheduled to preach. As he proceeded out of the door, the Lord said, "Don't go."

Festo argued with the Lord, "But I must."

The Lord replied, "Don't go."

Festo stuck to his guns. "I have to go. The people are waiting."

Then the Lord said, "You go on, but I will stay here with Mary." Festo stayed and put things right with his wife before he proceeded.

I try to spend a certain amount of time every day in quiet before the Lord. In the perfect world I will feel His presence, read His Word with full assurance of understanding and go out to do my job with great confidence. But it isn't always like that. In fact, it is not very often that I feel a great sense of God in my quiet time.

There is an old spiritual that asserts, "Every time I feel the Spirit moving in my heart I'll pray." The trouble with those words is that if I truly waited to feel the Spirit moving in my heart before I pray, I would pray very little. This is partly why Paul told us to "be prepared in season and out of season" (2 Tim. 4:2). For "in season" is when God's special presence is *felt*; "out of season" is when He chooses to stay behind—to see if we will put into practice the things we learned in His presence.

It takes greater faith and devotion to pray, trust and obey when God is absent than when He is present. I suspect we please God more by being faithful "out of season" than by being faithful "in season." More faith is required "out of season."

And without faith it is impossible to please God,

85

because anyone who comes to him must believe that he exists and that he rewards those who earnestly seek him.

—Hebrews 11:6

There is a sense in which we can get emotionally tied to the Lord in an unhealthy manner. This is partly why Jesus stayed behind. He was under His Father's orders and may not have known that He was doing it for this particular reason, but Joseph and Mary needed to develop a healthy detachment from Jesus. Jesus did this same thing later many times with His disciples. He sent out the Twelve (Matt. 10:5–15). Later He sent out seventy-two others, during which He was not personally at hand for those who went out (Luke 10:1–12). They needed to be on their own, as it were, to put into practice what they had learned personally from Jesus.

In another instance, He made the disciples get into a boat and "go ahead of him" (Matt. 14:22). He did not stay with the eleven disciples the whole time after His resurrection—for forty days Jesus would come and go. The special anointing of the Spirit is much the same. I am required to carry on whether or not I *feel* Him present. If I didn't carry on, I would never go out much at all. I would also be demonstrating that I had not learned much from His presence and His Word at all.

LEST WE TAKE OURSELVES TOO SERIOUSLY

The reaction that Joseph and Mary had when they finally found Jesus in the temple courts several days later is proof that they took themselves too seriously: "Son, why have you treated *us* like this?" (Luke 2:48, emphasis added). Focusing only on their own feelings, they became annoyed that Jesus had kept silent and did not inform them He was staying behind in Jerusalem.

I face this same problem nearly every day. One of my

greatest fears is that God will pass me by because I might take myself too seriously if He gave me a greater anointing. Taking oneself too seriously is assuming one is more important than he or she really is. It results in our expecting more respect and attention than is warranted. We begin feeling that we, more than anyone else, should be notified the moment God has new plans for His church—and, of course, those plans should include us.

Jesus demonstrated this point by His parable of the workers in the vineyard. All the workers had agreed on a stipulated sum of money for their contract to work. But those who turned up toward the end of the day received the same pay as those who had worked all day. This caused a lot of murmuring. "'These men who were hired last worked only one hour,' they said, 'and you have made them equal to us who have borne the burden of the work and the heat of the day'" (Matt. 20:12).

Those who had worked the longest, and possibly the hardest, expected to receive more. But the landowner answered, "'Friend, I am not being unfair to you. Didn't you agree to work for a denarius? Take your pay and go. I want to give the man who was hired last the same as I gave you. Don't I have the right to do what I want with my own money? Or are you envious because I am generous?' So the last will be first, and the first will be last" (vv. 13–16).

When we have worked long and hard, we begin to presume that our efforts will get the most recognition. But if others, who are Johnny-come-latelys, get this recognition and status, it gets our goat! And yet it only shows how self-righteous we are. When we get to heaven, I will not be surprised to learn that some of the disciples, such as Peter and John, initially resented the abundant grace given to Saul of Tarsus. Instead of divine wrath and judgment coming down on Saul's head, he received mercy and grace. The angels even may have said to God, "Aren't you going to punish this man, Saul of Tarsus?"

If they did, I'm sure God said, "I think I will just change Saul and give him a ministry." In reality, the apostle Paul was given more insight and understanding than all the rest! I do not think it was easy for Peter and John to step aside for Paul.

God has a way of putting each of us in our place. But if we truly affirm Him as a God of glory and sovereignty, we should be the last to be surprised when He chooses an unlikely vessel for His honor. God said to Moses, "I will have mercy on whom I will have mercy" (Exod. 33:19). We should not be upset when He demonstrates this sovereign right. At the end of the day, not a single one of us has a right to take ourselves too seriously. After all, God has shown mercy to us already!

Even when we are seeking to walk in obedience to the Lord there is a danger of taking ourselves too seriously. We may fall prey to the "Elijah complex." Elijah's finest hour was followed by his taking himself very seriously. "I am the only one left," he said, having earlier lamented he was no better than his ancestors. But God nonetheless manifested His glory in an unexpected manner—through a "gentle whisper." (See 1 Kings 19:4–12.)

The twin sins of *self-righteousness* and *self-pity* so readily lift their ugly heads in us. For example, it is a rare person who can be an intercessor in prayer and not boast about it. It is a rare person who can pray for a leader and then refrain from giving advice. It is a rare person who can be greatly used of God today and tomorrow be quietly willing to watch God use another. It is a rare person who can see God answer prayer on one item and not question because He doesn't answer other prayers. It is a rare person who can enjoy sweet intimacy with Christ today and not feel sad when He doesn't manifest

His presence tomorrow.

Few of us can handle much success, especially in the area of knowing God. God is the only one who can deal with us when we are like that. Sometimes the only way He can get our attention is by being ruthlessly silent. Don't fear His silence. Use it to examine your heart and motives. Listen expectantly for the silence to be broken by the glory of His manifested presence once again in your life.

CHAPTER FIVE

The Danger of Presumption

Thinking he was in their company, they traveled on for
a day.

—LUKE 2:44

I n late 1994 several British Christian leaders met in a
London hotel to pray about the "Toronto Blessing,"
as it was called. At the beginning of that year, the
Holy Spirit came down in an unusual manner at the
Airport Vineyard Church in Toronto, now called Airport
Christian Fellowship. This extraordinary phenomenon,
characterized largely by people falling on the floor and
laughing through the laying on of hands, made its way
to London, notably at Holy Trinity, Brompton. From
there it spread like wildfire all over London and Britain.
As a result, about thirty leaders came together for nearly
a twenty-four-hour meeting in a London hotel for
prayer and guidance. The group included leaders from

various streams. Some were in favor of the Toronto phenomenon, some against it and some fairly neutral.

We began praying around four o'clock on a Monday afternoon. We also listened as one or two papers were read from a historical perspective. I gave a brief talk, taken from Acts 2, on "What Is Revival?" We began praying corporately, and then divided into small groups to continue praying.

After we had been praying for only a short time, some of the leaders began circulating from group to group with a statement they were preparing. This statement was supposed to reflect what God had told us as a result of praying together for the better part of twenty-four hours. But we had only *begun* praying! It wasn't even supper time yet, and already a statement had been proposed to reflect our twenty-four-hour season of prayer!

I was a little surprised, but I didn't say anything. I hoped others would see what was obvious to me—some minds were made up before we began to pray. I wondered if the statement could have been written before the prayer meeting and issued without any prayer at all! I knew the statement did no harm and was drawn up with the best of intentions. And I knew it was a good thing that leaders of diverse backgrounds had actually met to pray. But I couldn't help thinking, *Did God really speak? Did we really hear from God? What was the point of meeting to pray to see what God would say if our minds were already made up before we began about what He would say?*

This situation reminded me of a pastor in Kentucky who was struggling with his church. Suddenly, out of the blue, he got a call to become the minister of a church in Hawaii. He said to his wife, "You pack while I pray about it." It is hard to seek the mind of the Lord when our own minds are already made up.

I was raised in a strict environment. I could not go to

places like a theater or the circus. Although the denomination in which I was raised was neutral on the issue of
"mixed bathing," as it was called (boys and girls swimming together), my dad wouldn't allow me to go. He felt
I would be tempted to lust if I saw girls around me in
their swimming suits. But I kept begging to go. Finally
my dad came up with a proposition for me: Would I pray
about it? Yes! So I did, and God told me it would be OK
to go!

It is to my dad's everlasting credit that he let me
go—and that he showed trust in my seeking the Lord.
But I also recall that I felt God say it was OK as soon as
I knelt to pray! I also suspect that God would have had
a difficult time convincing me otherwise. My mind was
already made up. That was not the last time I prayed
about something about which I was already persuaded. I
have learned that it is very hard to hear from God when
we are not truly open to what He may have to say.

We often presume that we already know God's will.
If we have known His special presence up to a certain
point, we easily assume that presence will stay with us,
especially if we are in our comfort zone. That assumption can get us into difficulty.

BEWARE OF PRESUMPTION

In this chapter we will focus on these words: "Thinking
he was in their company..." (Luke 2:44). The King
James Version says, "Supposing him to have been in the
company." It is an easy mistake to make, especially when
we are preoccupied with what seems right and true. Mary
Magdalene was looking at Jesus with tear-filled eyes,
"*thinking* he was the gardener" (John 20:15, emphasis
added). The same Greek word is used again when Peter
was miraculously delivered from prison—he "*thought* he
was seeing a vision" (Acts 12:9, emphasis added). Jacob

saw Joseph's coat stained with blood and presumed the worst. "It is my son's robe! Some ferocious animal has devoured him. Joseph has surely been torn to pieces" (Gen. 37:33). But Joseph was still very much alive.

Presumption is an easy thing to take on board. But in many cases it can be costly. It is so hard not to presume. *Presume* means to take for granted or to "suppose to be true." It is assuming something to be true without the evidence. I believe we should pray every day to avoid presumption. False assumptions have led many people into difficulty—and some to destruction. One of the most alarming proverbs is this: "There is a way that seems right to a man, but in the end it leads to death" (Prov. 14:12).

What did Joseph and Mary presume? They presumed that Jesus moved with them just because they moved. That was reasonable to presume at the time. There was no reason to think otherwise. But it was a lesson they never forgot. It could have been the most traumatic moment for Mary between Jesus' birth and His public ministry. It was the only event of that era that apparently she chose to share only with Luke. It does not appear in the other Gospels. She could have told hundreds of stories about Jesus' childhood years. But she revealed only this one.

From Mary's example, we can learn that we should not presume upon God merely because we have had a close relationship with Him. Nobody was closer to Jesus than His parents. That is about as close to the Lord as one could ever get! And if they made the mistake of presuming that Jesus moved because they moved, how much more should you and I be cautious in this area.

Worse than their presumption is ours when we fancy that we are closer to God than we really are. I often wonder, *Why does God hide His face from us—suddenly and without notice, especially after a time of great intimacy with*

Him? I think part of the reason is to keep us from being presumptuous.

Recall Isaiah's words: "Truly you are a God who hides himself, O God and Savior of Israel" (Isa. 45:15). I have tried to figure out why Isaiah placed those words in the forty-fifth chapter and not somewhere else. They don't seem to fit. But maybe that *is* the point—at an unexpected time, for no apparent reason, God chooses to hide His face. That means He disappears at times right after revealing Himself to us. His presence subsides with no apparent reason. It *could* mean we have grieved the Spirit. But it may also be because we need to be put in our place lest we get too familiar with God.

It is possible to develop an "overfamiliarity" with God after He has been showing Himself for a while, answering one prayer after another and giving us clear guidance. We begin to think we have a "handle" on Him. That is one reason He suddenly "withdraws the light of His countenance," as the Westminster Confession of Faith puts it. We must never forget:

> Do not be quick with your mouth,
>> do not be hasty in your heart
>> to utter anything before God.
> God is in heaven
>> and you are on earth,
>> so let your words be few.
>
> —ECCLESIASTES 5:2

Not only did Joseph and Mary presume that Jesus would move with them if they moved, but they also presumed that they were the ones to whom He would say anything important that He had to say. The truth is, He had a lot to say. But because Joseph and Mary were not where Jesus was, they missed entirely what He said. His words caused the professionals of Jerusalem to marvel, yet Joseph and Mary were upset.

I know what it is to feel angry with the Lord for speaking where I haven't been. When I feel I have been close to Him, and He to me, I like to think He will tell *me* if He is going to move powerfully, wherever it is. If I prove my love for God by putting my reputation on the line by hard decisions, does this not qualify me for being notified if the Holy Spirit is going to act powerfully somewhere? No, I am not automatically qualified.

The Son of God opted to remain silent with His parents when He had a ministry to the teachers at the temple. Jesus did not say, "Don't go back to Galilee without Me." He said nothing. This offended Joseph and Mary.

God may choose to say nothing to any of us. We must not sulk over His silence, but we must bend the knee to His right to inform or withhold information. He is sovereign.

Certain factors played a part in creating Joseph and Mary's presumption. One factor was familiarity—what they were used to. They knew their son well. They knew His ways—or thought they did. That was the problem. They were not prepared for Him to carry on in a manner with which they were not familiar.

Yet they knew important facts about Him no one else knew. They knew about His birth. They knew He had no human father, and should have come to the obvious conclusion then that He was the Son of God. Later when Jesus asked, "Didn't you know I had to be in *my Father's* house?", He implied that they should have known. But they apparently weren't ready for this sort of thing yet.

We are never ready. We all want to maintain the familiar relationship with the Lord we've had for so long. It becomes our comfort zone. Yes, we may have worked diligently to develop the relationship with God we have.

But we want it to stay *that way* from now on. We may well have moved out of a previous comfort zone to get to our present spiritual location—not even aware that the new place has become a *new* comfort zone!

DON'T LET YESTERDAY'S CONTROVERSY BECOME TODAY'S COMFORT ZONE

The victory steps we took yesterday for God through the storms of controversy can become the still waters of today's comfort zone. An example from early church history can demonstrate this principle. Early in the fourth century there was a storm of controversy raging about the Word of God. Arius, father of the Arian movement, had declared that Jesus was "like" God *(homoiousion)*, but not the same as God *(homoousion)*.

The matter focused on the usage of the Greek letter *iota*, or *i*, which was used to show that Jesus was merely "like" God. The Arians were winning the argument for years.

However, an early church leader by the name of Athanasius disagreed vehemently. "No!" he thundered, unflinchingly holding to his conviction that the Word (Jesus) was God—as much God as God the Father was God.

"The world is against you," the Arians said to Athanasius.

Flashing his black eyes, he shouted, "If the world is against Athanasius, then Athanasius is against the world." He bore the brunt of the controversy and eventually won the argument.

There is no controversy about the divinity of Jesus today—it has become a comfort zone to the believer. Who doesn't believe that Jesus is God—unless you are a member of a cult or one who denies the infallibility of Scripture?

This principle can be seen in thousands of examples

97

throughout church history. Many of our basic tenets of the faith were born out of the storms of controversy through tears and pain. We see this illustrated even in the biblical example of the Pharisees.

The Pharisees presumed they were the guardians of the ancient law—a law that had been honed through the storm of controversy and persecution by the ancient prophets from centuries before. They defended to the hilt the ancient teachings of the prophet Isaiah. But when the One about whom Isaiah prophesied came along, the Pharisees hated Him.

Jesus warned the Pharisees of the paralysis of this comfort-zone thinking:

> Woe to you, teachers of the law and Pharisees, you hypocrites! You build tombs for the prophets and decorate the graves of the righteous. And you say, "If we had lived in the days of our forefathers, we would not have taken part with them in shedding the blood of the prophets." So you testify against yourselves that you are the descendants of those who murdered the prophets.
>
> —MATTHEW 23:29–31

Upholding the ancient prophets was, to the Pharisees, merely being faithful to the Word. But their thinking had trapped them in a dangerous comfort zone and was hindering them from being able to recognize the very Messiah about whom Isaiah prophesied. We must never forget that the very people who rejected Jesus and sought His death were the religious leaders of His day, the ones who contended most fiercely for the expression of religious faith they presumed most accurate. We cannot expect to uphold the true honor and glory of God when we are merely sound in our doctrine but hostile to the way God is *applying* His Word today.

In the 1960s Arthur Blessitt started a coffeehouse ministry on Hollywood's Sunset Strip. He built a large wooden cross, which he nailed to the wall of his coffeehouse. God told him to take the cross down off the wall and carry it on foot around the world, which he did. He was later quoted as saying, "If I knew I was going to have to carry it around the world, I wouldn't have made it so big."

Countless thousands have come to Christ as a result of his pilgrimage with the cross. Heads of state have invited Arthur into their homes. He stayed in the house of Israel's Prime Minister Begin. He received the Sinai Peace Medal for his historic walk from Jerusalem to Cairo. He has spent time with Israeli generals, and also with Yasir Arafat.

I invited him to spend a month at Westminster Chapel during May 1982. As I look back at this time now, it was the most pivotal (and best) decision I have made since coming to Westminster. He turned Westminster Chapel upside down. We were forced out of our comfort zone.

It was hard. The result was the greatest internal crisis in Westminster Chapel's history. Although the storm of controversy raged for at least four years, we survived! When it was finally over, I said to myself, "No more controversies for me. I've paid my dues. I showed I would be obedient." I fully intended to carry on in my new comfort zone. But God had other ideas—and has confirmed to me several times that He believes I am safer *out* of my comfort zone.

In the case of Joseph and Mary, they wanted to maintain the relationship with Jesus with which they had become comfortable. As a result, they had paid a price—a severe price. They became the scandal of Nazareth. Jesus was rumored to be the illegitimate son of Joseph and Mary—who apparently couldn't wait to get married.

(See John 6:42 to read of a later time when this same rumor surfaced again.)

Joseph and Mary made a commitment not to tell what they knew about Jesus' true lineage. Even though their silence may have cleared their names, no doubt it fueled the controversy and caused them to be seen as letting down God's holy standards of purity. So they bore an immense stigma.

Since they went to Jerusalem every year for the Feast of Passover, they were obviously familiar with the custom. It had become a habit. It was part of their culture. Religious and spiritual though it may have been, it was all thoroughly familiar to them. They weren't expecting anything out of the ordinary to take place.

That, I fear, is where some of us are in our churches today. We keep the "feasts"—Christmas, Good Friday, Easter and other "holy days" on the church calendar. But nobody really expects anything to happen on those occasions that would be out of the ordinary. A couple of years ago I spoke on the subject "What If Revival Came at Christmas?" It didn't, but neither did anybody really expect it to come. It would have messed up everyone's plans had it come, including my own. I looked forward to opening presents, eating turkey, watching the celebrations over the media and my favorite movies on television.

The truth is, none of us are prepared for God to step in, take over, shock us and show up in a manner with which we are not familiar. When Arthur Blessitt first came to Westminster Chapel, a lot of people were upset. His message—and his method of delivering that message—seriously threatened our comfort zone as a church. But we had told God that we wanted revival more than anything else. "If this brings us closer to it, then we must accept feeling uncomfortable," I insisted.

When things went from bad to worse, one deacon

actually asked, "Do we *want* revival after all?" The implicit answer to his question was, No. Most of us will avoid genuine revival if we can.

Jesus' actions as a young boy at the temple during the time of Passover—after Joseph and Mary had had enough and wanted to get back to Nazareth—edged the Jewish people of His day closer toward true revival. True revival always includes the fact of people being astonished.

"When he was twelve years old, they went up to the Feast, according to the custom" (Luke 2:42). *Custom* is defined as "a usual way of behaving or of doing something." That is as good a definition as you will find for what we call a *comfort zone*.

That is often the way we expect church to be. Jack Deere has preached a thought-provoking sermon titled "Why Go to Church?" When I knew he was going to preach that sermon at Westminster Chapel, I was sobered a bit. I thought, *Yes, why do we go to church?* He gave new, refreshing reasons I hadn't thought of. I believe that if that which is out of the ordinary happened in our church services regularly, people would have different reasons for going to the services. Of course, some wouldn't go at all.

THE WORLD LONGS FOR THE AUTHENTIC

The world is crying for something out of the ordinary, as long as it is authentic. The world wants to see things like Jesus amazing the teachers of His day. When an authentic demonstration of Jesus' authority takes place, the world takes notice—and even notices when those *who seem to be closest* to Jesus are upset.

The Feast of Passover was a traditional Jewish ceremony. It was an essential part of the ancient Law and occupied a special place in Israel's tradition. Its observance was commanded lest people forget what God had done in 1300 B.C. when He delivered the people of Israel from the bondage of Egypt.

The Lord's Supper, which Jesus instituted as the ultimate fulfillment of the Passover, is given to us partly so we do not forget why He came and what He did for us. (See Matthew 26:17–29; 1 Corinthians 5:7.) But the Passover Feast that Jesus and His parents attended was upstaged by His extraordinary appearance as the Son of God. We should hope the same might happen when we partake of the Lord's Supper today.

The historic Cane Ridge Revival (1801), called America's "Second Great Awakening," really began as a result of one minister's bold openness to the Holy Spirit when his church was observing the Lord's Supper.

We are at home with a ceremony. The observance of weddings, funerals, baptisms, the Eucharist, ordinations and confirmations are defined as a "set of formal acts, especially those used on religious or public occasions."

Ceremonies like these are also characterized by "formal politeness." That is not exactly the way Mary treated Jesus after He had demonstrated a measure of His glory. People who are normally very polite can be the most outrageous and indignant when what was supposed to be ceremonial is upstaged. Think of the way Michal, King David's wife, reacted when she saw David "leaping and dancing before the LORD" when the ark of the covenant came to Jerusalem (2 Sam. 6:16). When Michal saw David's behavior, she responded sarcastically, "How the king of Israel has distinguished himself today, disrobing in the sight of the slave girls of his servants as any vulgar fellow would!" (v. 20). David discovered who his true friends were. An unexpected move of the Spirit has an interesting way of doing this.

FELLOWSHIP WITH—OR WITHOUT—JESUS?

One other factor characterized Joseph and Mary's comfort zone—familiar company. "Thinking he was in their company, they traveled on for a day" (Luke 2:44). There is no way of knowing how many made up the company of people traveling with Joseph and Mary. But almost certainly those traveling together had two things in common:

- They all had an interest in Jewish feasts.

- They were all from the same area, possibly Nazareth.

Company may mean companionship, a number of assembled guests or people with whom you spend time. Joseph and Mary presumed Jesus was in their company.

Koinonia is a Greek word for *fellowship*. "But if we walk in the light, as he is in the light, we have fellowship [*koinonia*] with one another, and the blood of Jesus, his Son, purifies us from all sin" (1 John 1:7).

We all need fellowship. We need each other. But what makes fellowship *koinonia* is the presence of Christ. *Koinonia* is translated "communion" in the King James Version when Paul discusses the Lord's Supper:

> The cup of blessing which we bless, is it not the communion of the blood of Christ? The bread which we break, is it not the communion of the body of Christ?
> —1 CORINTHIANS 10:16, KJV

It is through the usage of this Greek word that the observance of the Lord's Supper came to be known as *communion*. And *communion with Christ* is exactly what it should be. But this is only possible when Christ is recognized at our observances of the Lord's Supper.

It is a wonderful thing to know that Christ *is* present

when we have the Lord's Supper. Whether He is recognized or He manifests His glory in an unmistakable manner, He nonetheless is present when we come together in His name.

> For where two or three come together in my name, there am I with them.
>
> —Matthew 18:20

Jesus promised to be with us when we convene to eat and drink at His Table (Matt. 26:29). But it is extremely important that we recognize Him. Some of the Corinthians didn't, and they paid a severe price as a consequence. (See 1 Corinthians 11:30.)

Joseph and Mary thought—presumed—that Jesus was in their company. That company of people was their comfort zone. It was an area of familiarity. They saw the same people, faces, clothes, possessions. That was good enough. But Jesus wasn't there.

104

UNITED—OR DIVIDED?

I have often been amazed at how quickly a company can be divided, depending on how people react to the special manifestations of God's glory. The special presence of God unites and divides.

> Do not suppose that I have come to bring peace to the earth. I did not come to bring peace, but a sword. For I have come to turn "a man against his father, a daughter against her mother, a daughter-in-law against her mother-in-law—a man's enemies will be the members of his own household."
>
> —Matthew 10:34–36

The cross unites. It even unites enemies. "That day Herod and Pilate became friends—before this they had been enemies" (Luke 23:12). It is startling how the manifestation of God's glory brings people together who previously were not on speaking terms! I have seen it again and again. People who love what God is up to discover friendship and fellowship with people they had not truly known.

But the reverse is also true. The cross divides. It works both ways. For people who *reject* what God may be doing in a given time have a strange way of finding each other. They unite against God's manifestations. And likewise people who love it find each other.

But with Joseph and Mary presuming Christ to be with them, it turns out He wasn't. They trusted their comfort zone—the company—but He wasn't there. This also goes to show how precarious it is to look to people you know and take for granted that Christ is with them in an intimate sense. People you know and love may not have the intimacy with the Lord you may think they have. The discovery of how people *really* are (when it comes to a solid relationship with the Spirit of God) can be a most sobering enterprise. The warning for us all is this: Never presume that those you like or love have the same robust zeal for the things of God that you may have. You too may think, as Joseph and Mary did, that Christ is in your company of relatives and friends.

I believe that for some of us the Toronto Blessing became a comfort zone. In 1994 it possibly represented one of the most divisive controversies of the church of that century. Many who opposed it were vehemently opposed—some "lost their heads" to anger as much as those "laughing their heads off" as the phenomena from the Toronto Blessing swept through the world, including Holy Trinity, Brompton, here in England.

But today, praying with people in the way that once led to laughter is as natural as singing "O Come, All Ye Faithful" at Christmas. There is nothing particularly

105

wrong with turning yesterday's controversy into today's comfort zone. I comfortably uphold the doctrine of Athanasius. But we must not be deluded into thinking that continuing to sail in the storm of yesterday's controversy is the same as bearing the cross of Christ in the way He wants us to bear it today.

Like it or not, God often continues to "remain behind," as it were, to see whether we will notice His absence. That is His style, always staying behind to allow us to demonstrate with our actions that we still want His glory. Our big mistake comes if we presume that just because God's special presence once was with us, it will automatically still be with us. If we presume we already know what He is up to—and move on—we may discover we have left Him behind.

CHAPTER SIX

How We Can Become Insensitive to the Spirit

They seem eager to know my ways.

—Isaiah 58:2

When I was a boy, my dad always listened to a live radio broadcast (while he shaved and got ready for work) from the Cadle Tabernacle in Indianapolis, Indiana. Each morning at 6:15 A.M. came the opening song:

Ere you left your room this morning,
Did you think to pray?[1]

The theme of those lines was ingrained in me from my earliest days. My dad took this principle very seriously and always made a point of praying thirty minutes before going to work every day. He was not a clergyman, but a layman, and he had a prayer life that, I fear, puts most church leaders today to shame. The average church leader in Britain, according to a recent poll, spends only four minutes a day in quiet time!

While He lived on earth, Jesus passionately modeled this principle of prayer. According to Mark:

> Very early in the morning, while it was still dark, Jesus got up, left the house and went off to a solitary place, where he prayed.
>
> —MARK 1:35

According to Matthew, Jesus also prayed in the evenings:

> After he had dismissed them, he went up on a mountainside by himself to pray. When evening came, he was there alone.
>
> —MATTHEW 14:23

Jesus spent the night praying before He made the choice of the twelve apostles:

> One of those days Jesus went out to a mountainside to pray, and spent the night praying to God. When morning came, he called his disciples to him and chose twelve of them, whom he also designated apostles.
>
> —LUKE 6:12–13

If the Son of God needed to pray, how much more do we? I find it extraordinary that Jesus prayed. After all, He was the God-man. He kept His eyes constantly on the Father, never making a move without the Father's beckoning (John 5:19, 30). It is a mystery to me that Jesus prayed at all, but He did—possibly to ensure that He never moved ahead of the Father's will.

When we become insensitive to the Spirit, chances are we are unaware of it at first. It is like being asleep; we don't know we were asleep until we wake up. In the meantime, we are filled with our own ways. It is a most precarious position to be in. One way to avoid becoming insensitive to the Spirit is by guarding our relationship with Him. When we know we are hearing His voice and experiencing His presence, we should neither quench nor grieve Him.

I believe that Joseph and Mary would not have moved on without Jesus if they had kept their eyes fastened on Him all the time. If we keep our eyes on Jesus, we can be spared much regret.

Let's take a closer look at some of the ways we can move on without Jesus, thus repeating the mistake that Joseph and Mary made.

NOT EARNESTLY SEEKING THE MIND OF THE LORD CONSTANTLY

"In all your ways acknowledge him, and he will make your paths straight" (Prov. 3:6). This is a wonderful proverb and a wonderful promise. "All your ways" refers to anything pertaining to us. Some people worry that they should not bother God with small things. But, as Pastor Jim Cymbala puts it, "Don't worry about bringing small things to God, for with God everything is small!" After all, Jesus said, "Whoever can be trusted with very little can also be trusted with much, and whoever is dishonest with very little will also be dishonest with much" (Luke 16:10). It is much easier to bring the more difficult requests to God when we are in a daily habit of bringing *everything* to Him already.

> Oh, what peace we often forfeit,
> Oh, what needless pain we bear,
> All because we do not carry
> Everything to God in prayer![2]

One of the saddest moments in the life of Joshua came when the Gibeonites lied to and deceived Joshua and the Israelites. (See Joshua 9.) Before he died, Moses had warned the Israelites: "Make no treaty" with any of the inhabitants of Canaan (Deut. 7:1–2). But the Gibeonites ingeniously manipulated their way into Joshua's good graces, and before he realized what was happening, "Joshua made a treaty of peace with them to let them live, and the leaders of the assembly ratified it by oath" (Josh. 9:15). Soon afterward they realized they had been tricked. "But all the leaders answered, 'We have given them our oath by the LORD, the God of Israel, and we cannot touch them now'" (v. 19). Israel had the problem of the Gibeonites on their hands for years and years.

These difficulties happened because the Israelites "did not inquire of the LORD" (Josh. 9:14). Although they had the faithful means of knowing God's will at their fingertips, they bypassed this process and moved on without Him.

We do the same thing when we do not talk to God about everything. *Everything.* If God let Joseph and Mary and Joshua move ahead without keeping their eyes diligently on the Lord, none of us should be surprised when we get into unnecessary difficulty. I have even done things like accepting invitations and engagements I should have declined—all because I said yes too rashly. Often, when the time came to fulfill these obligations, I had to say, "Why ever did I agree to do this?" I now pray more carefully over every little opportunity that comes my way.

I am gullible, especially when it comes to flattery. If someone compliments my preaching, for example, I fear I am too often like putty in that person's hands. My wife used to warn me about one person in particular who would rush up to me after a service and boost me to the high heavens. "You'd better be careful about that man," she kept saying. Before I knew it, I accepted him for church membership—which turned out to be a tragic mistake. I have learned to listen not only to the Lord but also to my wife! I now pray daily about such things as invitations I accept and people I take into my confidence.

It does not follow that every single time I fail to know God's will clearly, He lets me do something stupid. He has graciously overruled my haste thousands of times and bailed me out—or mercifully led me all along. But I have now lived long enough to take seriously the matter of seeking the Lord earnestly and constantly in the big things and the small things.

Neither does it follow that every single time I seek the Lord in big and small matters I always get it right. Often I still find myself in situations that seemed so right—but turn out so wrong! It is hard to be neutral, or open, when something *seems* so right. It's even harder when we eagerly want something.

GOING BY SUBJECTIVE FEELINGS RATHER THAN GOD'S OBJECTIVE WORD

Feelings can be so deceptive. They are the product of all our wishes, fears, prejudices and past experiences. We may develop a "sixth sense" of what is right and wrong that can be very misleading. Even worse, we can truly be led of the Holy Spirit one day and *think* we are the next—and be wrong.

Joseph and Mary were led of the Spirit to take Jesus to the Feast of the Passover. By doing so they were following the Law. But once the Passover was finished, they jumped ahead, *thinking* Jesus was with them.

More than anyone else I have known, Arthur Blessitt taught me to offer the gospel to *everybody* indiscriminately. That was surely right, for Jesus tasted death for "everyone" (Heb. 2:9). But I had not taken seriously enough that "everyone" also means all *kinds* of people. Arthur led our congregation to begin speaking to people on the streets about their spiritual condition. We soon noticed that the people who stopped and listened to us were not always merchant bankers or members of the House of Lords. Our greatest number of converts were the homeless, tramps and beggars.

My subjective feelings had not led me to embrace this perspective gladly. Westminster Chapel had been a fairly middle-class church for most of this century. That suited me fine. But I was wrong to hope to perpetuate this. Jesus unveiled the scroll of Isaiah 61 and claimed the verses referred to Himself—thus reading His own mandate:

> The Spirit of the Lord is on me, because he has anointed me to preach good news to the poor. He has sent me to proclaim freedom for the prisoners and recovery of sight for the blind, to release the oppressed, to proclaim the year of the Lord's favor.
>
> —LUKE 4:18–19

112

God's objective Word has much to say about the poor and oppressed. I am ashamed to recall how often I played the role of the priest and the Levite who, seeing a man in trouble, "passed by on the other side" (Luke 10:31–32).

As I searched the Scriptures I read the following mandates from God:

> Defend the cause of the weak and fatherless; maintain the rights of the poor and oppressed. Rescue the weak and needy; deliver them from the hand of the wicked.
>
> —PSALM 82:3–4

> He who is kind to the poor lends to the LORD, and he will reward him for what he has done.
>
> —PROVERBS 19:17

> But when you give a banquet, invite the poor, the crippled, the lame, the blind, and you will be blessed.

> Although they cannot repay you, you will be repaid at
> the resurrection of the righteous.
> —Luke 14:13–14

When John the Baptist had second thoughts about Jesus being "the one who was to come," Jesus replied:

> Go back and report to John what you have seen and
> heard: The blind receive sight, the lame walk, those
> who have leprosy are cured, the deaf hear, the dead
> are raised, and the good news is preached to the poor.
> —Luke 7:22

Had you asked me prior to May 1982 whether we were trying to reach the poor, I would have honestly said, "Yes, but I don't feel *led* to emphasize that aspect of evangelism." My subjective feelings made me uncomfortable with reaching out to people like that. Not that we drove them away when they came to us; it is just that I wasn't *gripped* to try to reach people like that.

But today I know I wasn't listening to the Holy Spirit. The Holy Spirit has spoken objectively in His Word—whether I liked it or felt drawn in that direction or not.

Psalm 50:12 tells us this: "If I were hungry I would not tell you." Part of the meaning of that verse conveys the thought that God does not come down in an irresistible vision to tell us what He is feeling. Yet if we seek in His Word to discover God's needs, we discover that He *does* tell us when He is hungry—and thirsty, naked, sick and imprisoned! That is the message of Matthew 25:31–46.

One time a lady came up to Arthur Blessitt and asked, "Why is it that the Lord always seems to speak so clearly to you, but He never talks like that to me?"

Arthur replied, "Have you ever felt an impulse to talk to someone you didn't know about Jesus?"

"As a matter of fact I have," she answered.

Arthur looked at her and said, "Start listening to that

impulse, and the voice of the Lord will become clearer and clearer." The impulse of the Spirit, like the dove, is so gentle that we tend to underestimate it. But when it mirrors the objective Word, it is safe to obey it. The dividends are tremendous—an ever-increasing ability to recognize the Holy Spirit's promptings.

I know what it is to give my subjective feelings priority over God's objective Word—and feel good about it. For a period of time, I, for the most part, dismissed having to concentrate on the poor. I justified my thinking on the basis that *others* have a special calling in that area of ministry—and I didn't. In one sense my thinking was correct, of course. Westminster Chapel has not been called to be a rescue mission ministry for the homeless and poor. Our central calling is to preach the gospel. However, because I was not listening to the Holy Spirit's desires in this matter, we were not making a sufficient effort to reach every kind of person, regardless of culture or background, with the gospel.

Joseph and Mary walked toward Nazareth without Jesus and felt good about it because they hadn't missed Him yet. They allowed their feelings to dictate their actions. We often do the same, letting our feelings govern us and thus avoiding the hard sayings of Jesus. We do it with doctrine and with the practical teachings of the Bible. Early in our marriage I avoided tithing—and felt good about it—believing it was more spiritual to pay my debts to man rather than to God. Two years later we were *deeper* in debt. Our financial situation reversed only in proportion to our tithing! When I finally looked in God's Word—God's objective Word—the practical principle was right there. (See Malachi 3:10.) But my subjective feelings had won out, and I was the loser until I bowed to Scripture.

The list of examples as to how we prioritize our subjective feelings over the objective Word of God is long—I'm sure you can name several of your own. Our subjective feelings—more commonly known as our comfort zones—may camouflage as God's voice. I once asked a Mormon preacher if he would believe the Bible or the Book of Mormon if he had to admit that the two contradicted each other. He replied that he would have to go along with the Book of Mormon. I fear we do the same thing with our subjective feelings. Regardless of whether we are helping the hurting, paying our tithes, witnessing to strangers, refusing to listen to gossip, not giving in to grumbling or not pointing the finger and keeping a record of wrongs—all issues that relate clearly to biblical principles, so often we make decisions based on what we feel or think. Joseph and Mary began the trek back to Nazareth *"thinking* he was in their company." And we do this without realizing we have done anything contrary to God's thinking.

NOT BEING ACCOUNTABLE

It is my opinion that a chief reason people get off track is because they remain accountable to no one and feel good about it. "I am accountable to God alone," some piously say. That sounds good. But it isn't good at all. This is one of the best reasons for being a member of a church and under the authority of its fellowship and leadership. It is dangerous to make decisions based on a subjective feeling—"I don't feel led to get involved"—despite the objective warning God's Word has given us:

> Let us not give up meeting together, as some are in the
> habit of doing, but let us encourage one another—and
> all the more as you see the Day approaching.
> —HEBREWS 10:25

The truth is, we need each other. Many church leaders, including some high-profile Christians, imagine themselves exceptions to the rule. As a result, not just a few of these individuals have gotten into all kinds of difficulty, sometimes even falling into sexual sin. They feel they are above the spiritual judgment of those around them, and they put their confidence in nobody—except themselves. Many of the Christians who fall into sin are people who have not been accountable to people around them or over them.

All of us, from time to time, would like to think that we are the exceptions to the rule. It is easy to think that the temptations or trials we face are unique, and to assume that God will "let us off the hook" just this one time. Assuming such a thing is to believe the devil's lie. God's Word tells us this:

> No temptation has seized you except what is common to man. And God is faithful; he will not let you be tempted beyond what you can bear. But when you are tempted, he will also provide a way out so that you can stand up under it.
>
> —1 CORINTHIANS 10:13

God simply does not bend the rules for His people, not even the "best." This is why the Bible does not gloss over its heroes. King Saul became yesterday's man because he thought he was not accountable to anybody. King David, the only person in Scripture called a man after God's "own heart," thought he could get away with adultery, but was found out. (See 1 Samuel 13:14; Acts 13:22; 2 Samuel 12:1–12.) Are you accountable? Have you surrounded yourself with people who know you—and your motives for what you do—and will help keep you on the straight and narrow? I would urge you to be accountable to trusted friends and leadership.

Moses called the people of Israel to accountability many times. At one point, the men of the tribes of Gad and Reuben asked Moses' permission to take possession of the fertile lands on the east side of the Jordan River for their flocks and families. (See Numbers 32.) Moses reminded them that God had given instructions for the Israelites to take possession of the Promised Land on the west side of the Jordan. He also reminded them that God had instructed them to defeat their enemies in the Promised Land, and indicated that it would take all the tribes to do that.

Moses reached a compromise arrangement with the tribes of Gad and Reuben. If they would first do battle with all the Israelites to defeat the enemies and take possession of the Promised Land, then the men from Gad and Reuben could return to the east side of the river to live. The men agreed to Moses' plan. Then Moses called them to accountability with the following warning: "But if you fail to do this, you will be sinning against the LORD; and you may be sure that your sin will find you out" (Num. 32:23).

I know people who are in serious trouble because they have refused to be accountable. They will not listen to those who know them and love them. They get defensive at the thought that they should have to listen. Consequently, some reject their friends for a new set of friends who don't really know them. When those new friends begin to ask questions and require accountability, they too will probably be spurned.

When we reject suggestions or warnings, supposing that Jesus is in our company, we will be sorry—sooner or later.

ALLOWING BITTERNESS TO CREEP IN

Bitterness is a major cause of grieving the Holy Spirit. Paul admonished us:

And do not grieve the Holy Spirit of God, with whom

you were sealed for the day of redemption. Get rid of all
bitterness, rage and anger, brawling and slander, along
with every form of malice. Be kind and compassionate
to one another, forgiving each other, just as in Christ
God forgave you.

—EPHESIANS 4:30–32

Any sin—when being committed—seems somewhat
justified at the time. We sweep the filth under the
rug in order to carry on. But bitterness is possibly
the greatest deceiver of all. Talk about something
that seems right! Bitterness always has a cause—some
grievance or injustice. Whether it be from imperfect
parents, abuse, being lied about, being cheated on or
being let down by someone you fully trusted, we all
seem to have fairly strong reasons for feeling bitter and
holding a grudge.

I know what it is to feel bitter and feel good about
being bitter—and even think the Lord is in my company.
I'm sure you do, too. It can take years, or only seconds,
but eventually each of us has to face these hard truths:
Because of our bitterness, the Dove has quietly flown
away. And often we must also admit that the bitterness
was not warranted after all.

That's not to say that we didn't have been a cause.
You may have been betrayed or lied about by someone
whom you trusted. Maybe another Christian—even a
parent—has deeply hurt you. Perhaps some friends are
distancing themselves from you because they feel they no
longer need you. There are many circumstances where
bitterness can creep in. You may even think at the time
the hurt happens that you are quite right to be angry.

Mary was angry with Jesus! She demanded, "Son, why
have you treated us like this?" (Luke 2:48). Jonah was
angry with God for not vindicating his prophecy that

Nineveh would be destroyed. But the Lord asked Jonah, "Have you any right to be angry?" (Jon. 4:4). The answer was *no*.

Like it or not, the Dove will not adjust to us. If we want the Dove to remain, we must adjust to the Dove. This means *totally forgiving* those who hurt us. I believe the Lord's Prayer has made liars out of more people than any document in human history! Jesus told us to pray, "Forgive us our debts, as we also have forgiven our debtors" (Matt. 6:12). But does that make God responsible for what we say and do? No. We must adjust to the Dove and *mean it* when we pray, "Forgive us our debts, as *we also have forgiven* our debtors." A friend of mine has often said, "There is no forgiveness to the one who does not forgive."

When I pray to be forgiven, I am asking God to let me off the hook. When I, in turn, say that I have forgiven those who owe me, I have let *them* off the hook. When I pray *sincerely*, the Dove sweetly returns.

At the end of the day, all bitterness is ultimately directed toward God. We may say we are not bitter at God, but when we analyze our thoughts, we have entertained one of the following thoughts: *Why doesn't God deal with this horrible person?* Or, *Why did God allow this person to do this?* In other words, we want to know: *How could this thing happen to me?* It happened because God let it happen. He could have stopped it, but He didn't. Therefore, without trying to understand the plan of God, we blame Him—just as Mary and Jonah did.

Corrie ten Boom tells the moving story of how the very prison officer who had been so cruel to her beloved sister when she and her sister were imprisoned by the Nazis sat in the front row at one of her services. She noticed him just before she had to speak before the congregation. She cried out in her heart to God to be

119

filled with the love of Jesus. God overwhelmed her with His presence, and she spoke as planned. She spoke with the man after the service, and she found herself amazingly able to be gracious. The Dove remained.

Rodney Howard-Browne believes that people lose their healing and the blessing of joy (that sometimes comes from the laying on of hands) mostly because they cannot totally forgive someone who has hurt them. As a result, they get bitter. Because of their bitterness, their ailment returns and the joy subsides, and they wonder what happened.

Many a bitter minister manages to preach with apparent effectiveness because of three things:

- He knows his sermon very well.

- He has learned how to "appear" anointed.

- The gifts and calling of God are irrevocable (Rom. 11:29).

120

Because of these three factors, God uses their messages to touch others. But it is only a matter of time before these ministers will see that the Dove flew away much earlier. They will have to come to terms with the loss of the genuine anointing of the Holy Spirit. This principle is true with *all* Christians. We can play games only for so long.

When we keep a record of wrongs and point the finger, the Holy Spirit is grieved. (See 1 Corinthians 13:5; Isaiah 58:9.) We may not feel a thing—at first.

DOING WHAT IS "RIGHTEOUS" BUT NOT WHAT GOD REALLY WANTS

When Joseph and Mary took Jesus to Jerusalem, it was a righteous thing to do. So far, so good. But leaving Him behind was not right, even though they may have felt very good inside for having kept the requirements of the Law by observing the Passover in Jerusalem.

Isaiah addressed a similar malady:

> Shout it aloud, do not hold back.
>> Raise your voice like a trumpet.
> Declare to my people their rebellion
>> and to the house of Jacob their sins.
> For day after day they seek me out;
>> they seem eager to know my ways,
> as if they were a nation that does what is right
>> and has not forsaken the commands of its God.
> They ask me for just decisions
>> and seem eager for God to come near them.
> "Why have we fasted," they say,
>> "and you have not seen it?
> Why have we humbled ourselves,
>> and you have not noticed?"
>
> Yet on the day of your fasting, you do as you please
>> and exploit all your workers.
> Your fasting ends in quarreling and strife,
>> and in striking each other with wicked fists.
> You cannot fast as you do today
>> and expect your voice to be heard on high.
> Is this the kind of fast I have chosen,
>> only a day for a man to humble himself?
> Is it only for bowing one's head like a reed
>> and for lying on sackcloth and ashes?
> Is that what you call a fast,
>> a day acceptable to the LORD?
>
> —ISAIAH 58:1–5

The Israelites thought God was in their company because they were doing righteous deeds—like fasting. And yet, to their credit, they admitted that God took no notice of it. "'Why have we fasted,' they say, 'and you

121

have not seen it? Why have we humbled ourselves, and you have not noticed?'" (v. 3). The problem was, they enjoyed fasting and humbling themselves. It was like a game. Isaiah said that the Israelites of his day "seem eager for God to come near them" (v. 2). So many of us are like that. We seem eager for God to come down in power.

It is easy to get so busy in doing "righteous" things such as being active in church matters—and think that God must be thrilled. He may be nowhere near, but we carry on.

I think it is possible for God to be with us in one area and absent in another at the same time. For example, in my effort to make my way back to Jerusalem early in my ministry at Westminster Chapel, God dealt powerfully with me in certain ways. Initially He dealt with me in two significant areas: complaining and bitterness. The result was a fresh renewal of the Spirit in my personal life and public ministry. I became easier to live with at home, and my preaching improved some.

But there is another area of my life where I was, I fear, a failure. It has to do with my role as a father. I was doing "righteous deeds"—preaching, praying and, yes, fasting once in a while. Books emerged from the press. Some people claimed to be blessed by my preaching and writing. But I overlooked my family. I thought—"supposed"—that by putting my church and my ministry first I was putting God first.

I was living a paradox—God was with me in one area of my life, but He stayed behind in another while I moved on. There seemed to be a measure of anointing on my preaching, but I took our children for granted. I have paid a severe price as a result. I now think that had I put my family first, I would have preached just as well (probably better). It is only in recent years that I have come to terms with this. I can't get those earlier years back, and all I now know to do is trust God to restore "the years the locusts have eaten" (Joel 2:25).

This illustrates why I believe it is possible to experience the presence of Christ and His absence at the same time. Strange as it may seem, God can show His face and hide His face at the same time. He can be with me powerfully in one aspect of my life, yet allow the Dove to flutter away in another.

You may ask me, "Why didn't God *tell* you to spend time with your family?" He did. I didn't listen. I carried on. And yet He has proved to be with me in my ministry generally. It is not that God was not with Joseph and Mary as they moved ahead without Jesus. God loved them—and brought them back to Jesus. But we must be careful not to presume that God approves of all that we are and do merely because He is gracious to us in a particular area.

God isn't interested in our performance of certain righteous deeds—even though we enjoy doing them. He knows, and we must learn, that we often neglect what should be our priorities while concentrating on righteous deed-doing.

> Is not *this* the kind of fasting I have chosen:
> to loose the chains of injustice and
>   untie the cords of the yoke,
> to set the oppressed free and
>   break every yoke?
>
> Is it not to share your food with the hungry and
>   to provide the poor wanderer with shelter—
> when you see the naked, to clothe him, and
>   not to turn away from your own flesh and blood?
> —ISAIAH 58:6–7, EMPHASIS ADDED

These verses indicate that we must tune in to God's heartbeat. Doing so will almost always mean doing that

123

which requires more effort and may be (sadly) less fun in order to carry out His *whole* will.

FORGETTING TO THANK THE LORD

Joseph and Mary should have been the most grateful people on the face of the earth. What an honor—a privilege that could never be extended to anyone else— to be the parents of the one and only Son of God! I am sure they were aware of this, and they must have been in perpetual awe to be chosen for this service to God. But the fact that they could leave their child behind in the ancient capital of Israel shows that they, in some sense, took for granted His presence with them.

It is this sort of assumption that I suppose we all fall into. We take for granted the matter of showing grati- tude to God. When we are truly grateful, we will never let Him out of our sight—or move one inch without His conscious presence to the best of our ability.

But so glibly we say, "The Lord knows I'm thankful." Really? Then we should tell Him and show it.

In my own journey back to Jerusalem, I have been convicted of the need to be thankful in an ever-increas- ing manner. My first awareness of ingratitude really hit home when I was preaching through Philippians. Finally, I came to chapter 4, verse 6:

> Do not be anxious about anything, but in everything,
> by prayer and petition, *with thanksgiving*, present your
> requests to God.

The words *with thanksgiving* sobered me. I hadn't really done this. I have prayed tens of thousands of prayers and petitions to God without thanking Him. I will never forget something Dr. Lloyd-Jones once said to me in response to my comment, "But God already knows how I feel." The doctor said, "Tell Him!" Simple as that—tell Him.

I began doing that. I keep a journal, recording every eventful thing of every day of my life. I can tell you where I was at 3 P.M. on April 8, 1983. But after preaching on Philippians 4:6 (which, as it happens, was on November 13, 1988), I began a new thing—and have kept it up literally every day since. I re-read my journal of yesterday each morning—to remind me of what I did. I thank God for *every single thing I can think of* for which I'm thankful. It doesn't take long, less than a minute. But I do it.

Jesus healed ten lepers in one instant. One—only one—came back to say "thank you." "Jesus asked, 'Were not all ten cleansed? Where are the other nine?'" (Luke 17:17). That's a pretty strong hint about how much God cares and *notices* if we bother to thank Him.

Thanksgiving and praise lead to authentic worship, to a time when we are carried beyond ourselves and sense God Himself. It is a marvelous feeling. It begins with taking the time to say "Thank You" to God. This is another area of my own life where I needed to adjust to the Dove. Perhaps you need to do so, too.

NOT RECOGNIZING THE "BRUISED REED"

If I were to recount how often I have failed at this point, I fear that the number of times would almost overwhelm me with embarrassment. And yet there was a time in my life when I would not have even thought about this. But one day something happened that caused me to see how insensitive I was to sensitive feelings around me. I am one who has been at home in the fast lane. I seldom suffered fools gladly and often thought, *That should not bother this person.* It was no small breakthrough that forced me to notice a bruised reed before my eyes. "A bruised reed he will not break" (Matt. 12:20). Learning to do so changed my life. I discovered that this verse

125

means that God will not hurt the person already hurting—and I must not do so, either.

It's hard for me to think about how many times I caused the Dove to fly away by not being sensitive to the bruised reed. The *bruised reed* is a person who has been severely damaged—let down, deeply offended, deprived of love, misunderstood, neglected, criticized, or abused (whether verbally or physically). These persons may have carried the bruise for many years, or it may only have been there for a short time. But as a result, they are crying out for love—desperate just to be accepted for once.

However, from a fear of not being accepted, they manifest behavior that turns others off. But that is just their way of revealing their bruise. Perhaps they are hypersensitive and not pleasant to be around. The list is endless of ways they may manifest the bruise. There are bruised reeds all around us. The chances are, you can find one when you look in the mirror.

We can become insensitive to the Spirit by not recognizing the bruised reed that God puts in our path. We are all bruised reeds, and when we begin to treat people as such, we will become just a little bit more like Jesus.

God is pouring His mercy into our lives when we sense our insensitivity to the Spirit. For in that moment we are beginning—at last—to become sensitive to Him. If we come to terms with our insensitivity to the Spirit, we are demonstrating that we have not yet become so insensitive that we cannot hear Him.

CHAPTER SEVEN

Recognizing God's Absence

Then they began looking for him.

—Luke 2:44

I t might seem extraordinary that Jesus' parents traveled on for a day without recognizing He was not with them. But their company included relatives and friends, and His parents assumed that Jesus was part of the group. We don't know if they walked or traveled by a camel caravan. But we do know that the return home was routine—they traveled back and forth from Nazareth to Jerusalem as least once a year. Routine of habit, if anything, made it rather easy to carry on without Jesus. They were familiar with the territory, which also made it easy to move on without Him.

Routine of habit, even a good habit, often becomes a comfort zone. We all have comfort zones—and there is nothing wrong with them. But there is an inherent danger with them—familiarity with the way we've always done things can be misinterpreted as evidence of the special presence of God.

Take daily devotions, or quiet time, for example. Nothing is more important than a regular time with God. Moreover, it is a righteous thing to do. But because we are all self-righteous by nature, we can become defensive and closed. I have known people who bristle at a word from God—especially if it comes from outside their comfort zone. They think to themselves, *I am so close to God, and I regularly spend time with Him. I would have recognized immediately that this manifestation was authentic if it had really come from God.* Some of God's "best" people have rejected what God was saying simply because they assumed their walk with God was so orderly that it was impossible for them not to know it when God was speaking.

128

Our quiet time with God can serve as a defense mechanism to keep us from hearing an uncomfortable word from the Lord. This happens when we tend to do all the talking as we wait before the Lord. We may unwittingly run ahead of the Lord—especially when He chooses to be silent or absent, and because we are talking so much we don't notice.

It is an easy thing to do. For some time I was slow to accept words from God that made me uncomfortable. I was too smug, too sure I knew just what God would always do. Smugness is a feeling of self-satisfaction. It is an attitude that is very hard to penetrate. For this reason, we should plead with the Lord to help us to be more and more sensitive to the Spirit. Otherwise He may back away from us unobtrusively and let us move on, perhaps only to see how far we will go before we recognize His absence.

HOW LONG BEFORE WE
KNOW HE'S GONE?

How long does it take to recognize the absence of the presence of God? Luke tells us that "they traveled on for a day." Then they realized something was wrong. Luke does not tell us about the moment they became aware of Jesus' absence. Perhaps they were ready to settle in for the night or getting ready for the evening meal. Whenever it arrived, it must have been a sobering moment.

Routine of habit is generally a good thing. That discipline gets us up each day at a certain time to get to work on time. We know how long it takes to get to work, so we leave home accordingly. We need discipline to take time to read the Bible and pray. When it comes to church participation, routine of habit is also necessary in many ways. It gets us to the services on time. The familiarity of the start and style of worship and liturgy facilitates our response in worship.

But God could be absent and never be missed because of familiar routine. Even the most nonliturgical services have a predictable pattern. For years I attended a little church in Bimini, Bahamas. Compared to the Episcopal and Catholic churches on the island, this church was antiliturgical. But their pattern was as predictable as any I know. The minister always began, "Say praise the Lord! Say thank You, Jesus." That was their comfort zone, and I suspect that God could be absent and not be missed.

Jacob had the opposite problem. One evening God met with him unexpectedly, and his life was never quite the same again. He stopped for an evening's rest at some little water hole in the desert, never expecting anything important to happen to him there. But his encounter with God caused him to exclaim, "Surely the LORD *is* in this place, and I was *not* aware of it" (Gen. 28:16, emphasis added). He named that place *Bethel*—a place that has

129

remained on the maps since that moment because of God's intervention.

There seems to be two possibilities—opposite patterns—that may take us unawares:

- God being present and we not know it
- God being absent and we not know it

It is reasonable to ask the following questions: How long does it take to recognize God's presence? How long does it take to realize He is not present? Either question may come out of the desire to use spiritual discernment in each situation we face as believers.

One of the gifts of the Spirit is the ability to distinguish between spirits (1 Cor. 12:10). Some people assume that this means only the ability to recognize the demonic. This is a lopsided emphasis. For it also, if not primarily, means the ability to recognize the genuine Holy Spirit. It is one thing to be an "expert" in the area of the demonic—quite another to be able to discern the genuine presence of God. If anything, it takes a higher level of spirituality to recognize the *real* than it does to detect the counterfeit. But sadly there are people who think only in terms of recognizing the devil and seeing a demon behind every bush! It is just as important to discern when God is present as when Satan is active.

EXPERIENCING GOD'S PRESENCE

We cannot really discern God's absence until we have experienced His presence. Could it be that some Christians have not really experienced the special presence of God? Therefore they do not have a clue what is meant by His absence.

The manifestation of God's presence can be unveiled

in more than one way.

Jacob felt the presence of God at Bethel, and he was *afraid* (Gen. 28:17). For some there is a bias in the direction of the fear of God, which, to them, proves that God is present. Some people are even uneasy with joy. *Fear* is their comfort zone. They have a ready-made theological rationale for not smiling and looking sad instead. When we don't have much joy, we can hide behind the convenient view that God's glory always produces a sense of fear. That feeling of awe was what people experienced as a result of a healing presence in Galilee (Luke 5:17, 26). They felt this immediately after Pentecost (Acts 2:43) and following Ananias and Sapphira's being struck dead by the Spirit (Acts 5:11).

In Ezra's day, when the builders laid the foundations of the temple of the Lord, many "shouted for joy" (Ezra 3:12). When Ezra gave an exposition of the Law, Nehemiah said, "Go and enjoy choice food and sweet drinks, and send some to those who have nothing prepared. This day is sacred to our Lord. Do not grieve, for the joy of the LORD is your strength" (Neh. 8:10).

David said, "You will fill me with joy in your presence" (Ps. 16:11). The angel of the Lord said to shepherds, "I bring you good news of great joy" (Luke 2:10). As a result of Philip's preaching in Samaria, "there was great joy in that city" (Acts 8:8).

I recall a man at my old college in Nashville who stood up—right after singing "When I Survey the Wondrous Cross"—and shouted, "Let's stop singing these dead songs and get some life in this place."

We must try to remain open to the manner in which God chooses to manifest His glory. We can become so firmly entrenched in our specific comfort zone that we fail to recognize the presence of God. At the end of the day, it is impossible to describe adequately the feeling

131

of God's special presence—however it is manifested. As Ena Dickinson, a member of our congregation, put it, "It is impossible to describe a good prayer meeting." You have to *be* there. So it is with God's special presence.

I attended a service at Jackie Pullinger's church in Hong Kong. Some of it was in Chinese, some in English. But I could not stop weeping. Why? I don't really know. I just cried and cried. The first time I attended a service conducted by Rodney Howard-Browne I felt a sense of awe. People were laughing—hundreds and hundreds of people—all over the auditorium. Rodney wasn't even preaching, only leading worship. I was enthralled with the sheer presence of God. It happened again in one of Rodney's services in New Orleans. I wept and wept as people all over the auditorium laughed and cried. I would have given almost anything if my own church members could have been transported to that service. I knew I could never truly describe it.

The special presence of God is greater than anything said about it. But you won't miss it if you haven't experienced it. And you can believe it's still present after it has departed. Yesterday's memory of His presence and today's expectancy that it will be present can make you think God is present when He isn't. It is an easy mistake to make.

All revivals come to an end. All special manifestations of God's glory and presence come to an end. It does not follow that we have done anything wrong. "It is good for us to be here," Peter exclaimed when the Lord Jesus manifested His glory on the Mount of Transfiguration (Matt. 17:4). But that experience ended, and they had to come down from the mountain in order to move into the next phase of God's strategy and purpose (v. 9).

It is foolish to think God's special presence continues to be manifested when it isn't. And yet the *absence* of God's special presence can be most painful when it has been truly experienced. As I prayed one morning in March 1993 in our living room, I was discouraged beyond any level I had known. I had been going through an extremely painful time. That morning I sought the Lord as on any other day—but that day I was really desperate.

God came, in the most powerful sense of His presence I had known in years. An old Nazarene preacher, known affectionately as Uncle Buddy Robinson, used to talk about God "dropping a chunk of honey in my soul." God gave me honey that morning, and it lasted all day. While it was at its height I was determined, if possible, to keep that presence. I looked high and low in my heart, mind, life and experience to see how I could keep this. There was a residue the following day, but by the third day it had almost totally diminished. I tried for a day or two to tell myself it was like it was, but I came to terms with its absence.

Not that God left me—or was grieved with me (so far as I could tell). He just remained behind, and I had to go looking for Him. I do know that there was a lot in me that needed looking into. I have had to admit to a lot of bitterness I didn't know was still present. I could see a lot habits that needed changing, particularly regarding my family life. I wanted the Dove to adjust to me.

Two close friends in the Florida Keys, who happen to be professional bonefishing guides, entered into a prayer covenant with me. Each day I pray a particular matter each of them asked me to pray for, and they do the same for me. I asked them to pray daily for me to become more sensitive to the Holy Spirit. It is thrilling to me to know that every day of the year, John Sutter and Harry Spear are praying "that R. T. will become more sensitive to the Holy Spirit."

Their commitment to pray for me has made a profound difference in my life. Within a matter of months, I began to notice unusual changes take place in me that were needed. As an example, I became intrigued with this verse: "If I were hungry I would not tell you" (Ps. 50:12). It hit me powerfully one day that God was telling us He could be hungry! Suddenly the thought hit me that perhaps this is one way God tests our earnestness. As I pondered on this verse, I believe God revealed to me that it was a clear invitation to experience God where others never would. If God saw my earnest desire to experience His presence, perhaps He would tell me—and others who seek Him earnestly—when He was hungry. I began to connect this verse with the truth of Matthew 25:44, which asks, "Lord, when did we see *you* hungry or thirsty?"

There is a thread of truth in Scripture that I have called (for want of a better phrase) "The Divine Tease." This is when God says or does the opposite of what He feels—only to see our reaction. God "sets us up" with a test. He first disguises His presence and purpose in order to reveal our real feelings. The Divine Tease is designed to reveal what we are. Of course, God is not learning anything new about us, but He is testing us in order for us to see ourselves—and sometimes for others to see us—as we really are.

Jesus did this to the two people on the road to Emmaus, acting "as if he were going farther." When they urged Him to stay with them, He did—which actually is what He wanted all along. (See Luke 24:28–29.)

Jesus did this when the disciples were alone in a storm on the lake—He came walking on the lake and "was about to pass by them." But they cried out to Him, which was precisely what He wanted them to do. (See Mark 6.) When Jacob wrestled with the angel, the latter said, "Let me go, for it is daybreak." But Jacob replied, "I will not let you go unless you bless me" (Gen. 32:26). That is what God wanted despite the words, "Let me go." It was a pivotal moment for Jacob. The angel said, "Your name will no longer be Jacob, but Israel, because you have struggled with God and with men and have overcome" (v. 28).

Many of us would have let Jesus carry on down the road to Emmaus or let Jesus pass by on the water (assuming it was a ghost), or given in to the wrestling angel. In the same way we sometimes assume that if God were hungry He wouldn't hint otherwise. Recognizing His presence begins with recognizing His *ways*. "They have not known my *ways*," lamented God (Heb. 3:10, emphasis added).

This is why we should want to be more and more sensitive to the Spirit. As we are more sensitive to Him, we will more quickly recognize God's special presence—and absence.

Only Samuel knew that King Saul was yesterday's man (1 Sam. 16:1). Samuel recognized the direction in which the Sovereign Redeemer was moving, and then moved in that direction. We must be the Samuels of today. The people of Israel would not have recognized that Saul had lost the anointing of the Spirit. He wore the crown. He had the glory and prestige. He also had the following. He had the gifts—he even continued to prophesy! (See 1 Samuel 19:23–24.) Saul wore the crown but lost the anointing (1 Sam. 18:12). David had the anointing without the crown (1 Sam. 16:13). David developed a great sensitivity to the Spirit, which helped partly to ensure that he would not succeed before he was ready. (See 1 Samuel 24:5.)

Many of us are fooled by fanfare, hype, big crowds, oratory, lively worship and the excitement of people. I once watched a man pray for people. Each time he preceded his prophecy or word of knowledge with the words, "No hype, no hype—just watch God work!" But it seemed to me that it was nothing but hype.

135

The greatest freedom is having nothing to prove. This means that one doesn't have to make any claims at all if God really is at work. Shouting "No hype, no hype" is the same as protesting too much, as Shakespeare put it. Claims of revival and of spectacular works of God have caused many sincere people of God to think the Spirit was truly at work. However, a close examination of so many of these claims leads one, sadly, to conclude that God is, in fact, quite absent.

Whether the things you do consist of *true religion* or *natural* (or *fleshly*) *religion* depends on who initiated what you do—yourself or God. "Unless the LORD builds the house, its builders labor in vain. Unless the LORD watches over the city, the watchmen stand guard in vain" (Ps. 127:1). We can build a superstructure of wood, hay and straw, which some will think is a building made of gold, silver and precious stones. (See 1 Corinthians 3:11–15.) But it is only a matter of time until someone will say, "God wasn't in it at all."

The ancient prophet put it in this way: "'Not by might nor by power, but by my Spirit,' says the LORD Almighty" (Zech. 4:6). In this case the prophet was speaking of *natural* might and *fleshly* power—that which has but a natural explanation at the end of the day.

Deception is the worst thing that can happen to any of us. Yet Jesus warned that it would happen to many of us: "Many false prophets will appear and deceive many people" (Matt. 24:11). Paul spoke of God sending "a powerful delusion" so that some people would "believe the lie"—all because they refused to love the truth (2 Thess. 2:11).

I was named after my father's hero, Dr. R. T. Williams. When Dr. Williams preached an ordination sermon to new ministerial candidates, he gave them this counsel: "Honor the blood, and honor the Holy Ghost." By "honor the blood" he meant we must preach the cross of Christ, the atoning blood, and never underestimate how much God honors His Son's blood. By "honor the Holy Ghost" he meant having the discernment to recognize His presence, being willing to give in to the Spirit whenever He showed up in a special way. If necessary, this means forgetting your sermon and allowing God to work.

I saw this happen once. When I was a teenager, an evangelist came to our church in Ashland, Kentucky. He preached every night for two weeks. Every evening seemed better than the one before, every sermon a little more powerful. Crowds increased, expectancy was high. Then came the final service. I remember sitting on the front row—I could take you to the very spot. All eyes were fastened on the visiting preacher as he read his text. But after he read it, he said nothing further. There was quiet. Then tears filled his eyes, and he began singing a chorus I've known all my life:

> Wonderful, wonderful, Jesus is to me;
> Counselor, Prince of peace, Mighty God is He.
> Saving me, keeping me, from all sin and shame;
> Wonderful is my Redeemer, praise His name.[1]

My reaction was disappointment. *Is he only going to lead us in singing?* I wondered. Then he proceeded:

> Wonderful, wonderful...

By this time I was getting annoyed. Even as a teenager I wanted to hear his sermon. But he never preached. As he sang that chorus for the third time, dozens got up out of their seats spontaneously and ran to the altar, falling down sobbing and praying. I will never know what that sermon would have been like. I only know now that he was following R. T. Williams's counsel—he honored the Holy Ghost rather than deliver his sermon.

When you have been in services like that, it is easier to discern God's absence. When you have seen the Spirit truly work, you can also more easily detect the flesh at work.

It is therefore as essential to recognize God's absence as it is His presence. If we can do this, we are spared getting on a bandwagon that will lead us to disillusionment.

HOW DO WE RECOGNIZE HIS ABSENCE?

In order to come to terms with God's absence, we must be able to distinguish the signs that indicate He is gone. How then do we recognize His absence? The following indicators are sobering proofs that the Dove has *already* fluttered away.

ANXIETY

Mary revealed her anxiety when she said, "Your father and I have been anxiously searching for you" (Luke 2:48). We have all been like that, even in the presence of God—but not in His special presence, when the Spirit is *at home* in us.

"Ungrieved" is truly the way it is in His special presence. There we experience a peace that "transcends all understanding" (Phil. 4:7). It is God's own peace. This peace is different than peace *with* God, which assures us that we are His and are accepted (Rom. 5:1). God promises us a peace that is even greater than peace *with* Him. It is the peace *of* God that "transcends all understanding." The prophet Isaiah spoke of this peace: "You will keep in perfect peace him whose mind is steadfast, because he trusts in you" (Isa. 26:3). This is why Paul counseled, "Do not be anxious about anything" (Phil. 4:6). It seems ridiculous that we could live above anxiety—until one has experienced such peace.

When I experienced God's absence, I also experienced the loss of the peace *of* God. It was the loss of an actual

138

physical feeling—a feeling of inner rest. I had known a time of no anxiety whatever, no fear, just calm inside. It was extraordinary. Suddenly it was gone. I could not regain it by reliving it or by speaking of it to some close friend. The memory was pleasant to talk about, but it didn't bring the peace of God back to me.

When we live in God's special presence, we do not have to live in anxiety. God has not given us a "spirit of fear" (2 Tim. 1:7, KJV). A *spirit of fear* best describes anxiety. One possible difference between fear and anxiety is that you probably know what you fear, but anxiety—a spirit of fear—is a general state of mind where you can't put your finger on what you are afraid of. It is what almost certainly emerges in our hearts when God's special presence subsides. It is precisely because Christ's special presence is available to us that Paul could say, "Do not be anxious about anything," and, "Let nothing move you" (Phil. 4:6; 1 Cor. 15:58). When that sweet anointing settles on us, our problems disappear, and "not a blast of hurry touch the spirit there."

The experience I had in my car on October 31, 1955, was preceded by a most dreadful anxiety. I felt panic as I prayed and prayed. Then two verses came into my head:

> Casting all your care upon him; for he careth for you.
>
> —1 PETER 5:7, KJV

> My yoke is easy and my burden is light.
>
> —MATTHEW 11:30

The latter verse certainly *didn't* describe me. I pleaded for grace to cast all my care, all my anxiety, on the Lord in the hope that I might be able to say, "My yoke is easy and my burden is light." God came, and the peace was incredible.

IRRITABILITY

"Son, why have you treated us like this?" His mother asked (Luke 2:48). She was clearly annoyed and irritated. Whenever we are in this agitated state, it is a dead give-away that the Dove has flown away or, as in this case, stayed behind. Once the Spirit withdraws His special presence, in a sense we are left to ourselves. Soon our natural capabilities manifest. Almost certainly irritability will be one of them.

Some people may justify their irritability by calling it "righteous indignation." They may even point to the example of Jesus' anger in the temple to prove their point. (See John 2:15). It might be said this was what Mary showed.

I doubt it. Mary lost presence of mind and showed herself to be thoroughly human—just like the rest of us. While it is to Mary's credit that she divulged this humanity to Luke, it does not justify her annoyance. But it clearly illustrates our state of mind when the Dove is not calmly perched on us. When the special presence of the Spirit governs us, we are more likely to be in control of our words.

Love is not "easily angered" (1 Cor. 13:5). We may still become annoyed when we love, but not easily. We are not impervious to mistreatment, but we are less likely to react negatively when we are filled with the Spirit.

My point is this: When we are irritable, we should take it as a sign we have been left to ourselves, as it were, and consequently call out to God for mercy in order to find grace in this time of need. If we speak out while in an agitated state, it will come out wrong every time! Dr. Lloyd-Jones once gave me this advice: "When you are agitated, don't speak." If we see irritability as a red light—and stop, we can be spared regret. If we face our irritability and refuse to utter a word, there is the hope that, mercifully, the Dove will return, and with Him, the presence of the Spirit's mind—love that casts out fear (1 John 4:18).

CONFUSION OR MUDDLED THINKING

When His parents saw Jesus, they were astonished and asked, "Why have you treated us like this?" (Luke 2:48). They accused Jesus of treating them in an unfair manner because He stayed behind in Jerusalem. They took it personally. They focused on themselves.

Joseph and Mary panicked, which always leads to unclear thinking. The Holy Spirit always thinks clearly, and when we are Spirit-filled we will reflect clear thinking. We will not take rejection personally or see ourselves as the center of what is going on. The Holy Spirit is self-effacing, speaking "only what he hears" from the Father (John 16:13). Jesus did the same (John 5:19).

God never panics. The degree to which we have the mind of the Spirit will be the degree to which we reflect His calm and gentleness. Clear thinking will demonstrate sound judgment, wisdom and also truth in doctrine. "If anyone chooses to do God's will, he will find out whether my teaching comes from God or whether I speak on my own" (John 7:17). The ungrieved Spirit in us is the greatest preservative against theological error. Panic throws our thinking about biblical truth into disarray, and sadly, we sometimes foolishly defend propositions that have no warrant in Scripture. There is, therefore, a close connection between our personal relationship with the Holy Spirit and what we believe. If we come to the calm that characterizes God Himself, we will be led to truth.

It is an awful feeling to be left to ourselves without the aid of the Spirit. It has happened to me—publicly. In our church's greatest crisis many years ago, I was conducting a church meeting in which my leadership was under

141

question. I was not prepared for what was being said. I allowed the meeting to get out of hand, and those who opposed my ministry got the upper hand. Nothing that came out of my mouth was inspired. I never felt so deserted. As people left the meeting—some with a look of glee on their countenances—I knew I had failed to demonstrate the presence of the mind of the Spirit.

I was all right the next day. Clear thinking returned, and I was able to anticipate even greater challenges soon coming. But why did the Lord "stay behind" the night before? I do not know. But I learned not to pretend that I had the mind of Christ when I didn't. It taught me to know that the absence of clear thinking is the absence of God's special presence.

NOT RECOGNIZING THE LITTLE FOXES THAT SPOIL THE VINES

There is a curious verse in the Song of Solomon: "Catch for us the foxes, the little foxes that ruin the vineyards, our vineyards that are in bloom" (Song of Sol. 2:15). Before I bring this chapter to a close, I want to share what I have learned about grieving the Spirit. I do this with the hope it will help others to avoid unnecessary pitfalls that indicate the withdrawal of God's special presence. I now pray about the things I list below all the time. They are some of the things that I have learned will grieve the Spirit in my own life. When these things are present in my life, I have discovered that God's special presence is absent:

- *Self-pity.* Feeling sorry for ourselves always seems right at first, but we should never give in to it if we cherish the presence of the Dove.

- *Self-righteousness.* This is the identical twin of self-pity. We reflect on our obedience and fancy that God is giving us a little pat on the back.

Before we know it, we let our left hand know what our right hand is doing (Matt. 6:3). As a result, the Dove leaves.

∾ *Defensiveness.* This is not merely being "touchy"; it is the natural instinct to resist any criticisms. It is the opposite of turning the other cheek (Matt. 5:39). Love is partly "letting be." It is letting another point the finger at us and keeping quiet about it. It isn't easy, but the thought of losing God's special presence is sufficient motivation to let people say what they will.

∾ *Seeking a compliment.* "Let another praise you, and not your own mouth; someone else, and not your own lips" (Prov. 27:2). I know what it is to hint for a bit of praise, especially after having to make a hard decision or after preaching a sermon. I too have yearned to know, "How did I do?" I've tried very subtly to angle for a little feedback—and inwardly felt God's special presence subside. He knew what I was doing, even if others didn't. In reality, they probably knew, too.

∾ *Listening to gossip.* I am not sure which is worse—telling another "the latest" or listening to it. It is hard not to listen, especially if it is delicious bad news about someone we find threatening. But it so easily grieves the Holy Spirit.

∾ *Talking too much.* "When words are many, sin is not absent, but he who holds his tongue is wise" (Prov. 10:19). John Wesley often said that for every hour we spend talking, we

143

should spend two hours in prayer! I know how easy it is to begin in the Spirit and end up in the flesh when in conversation. (See Galatians 3:3.) At some point the Dove slips away, and we are coping as if alone.

❧ *Rushing.* Getting in a hurry—what Joseph and Mary did—almost always moves us ahead of the Spirit. The Holy Spirit is not in a hurry. "This is what the Sovereign LORD, the Holy One of Israel, says: 'In repentance and rest is your salvation, in quietness and trust is your strength, but you would have none of it'" (Isa. 30:15).

❧ *Pointing the finger.* "Do not judge, or you too will be judged" (Matt. 7:1). Pointing the finger in judgment invariably includes keeping a record of wrongs—which the Bible advises us not to do (1 Cor. 13:5). Doing so will result in the departure of the Spirit's special presence—probably before we complete our first negative comment about another person.

144

When we come to terms honestly with the absence of God's special presence, we are more likely to be in a position to find Him. But when we justify things—simply because it is easier to presume that God is with us—it hints of pigeon religion, something about which we will learn in the next chapter.

CHAPTER EIGHT

Pigeon
Religion

Are you so foolish? After beginning with the Spirit, are
you now trying to attain your goal by human effort?
—GALATIANS 3:3

igeons and doves are in the same family and look
much the same. But the pigeon is not the symbol
of peace. It was not a pigeon that came down and
remained on Jesus. The turtledove—symbolizing
the Holy Spirit—is different than pigeons in some
interesting ways.

It seems to me that many of the claims to the presence of the Dove among us are nothing but *pigeon religion*—a counterfeit for the Holy Spirit. In my own haste,
I have presumed the presence of God in my life many
times—when it was not the Dove after all. Often it has
been a pigeon—not the heavenly Dove—that gave me a
"religious" feeling.

My friend Pete Cantrell is an experienced expert in the area of pigeons and turtledoves. His observations have amused and gripped me. Their relevance for this book is almost astonishing. "Do you see that pigeon?" he said to me. "Watch him, he's getting ready to bully the pigeon next to him because it is perched on the spot he wants for himself." Seconds later, I watched it happen. "I don't see that happening with turtledoves," Pete added. "Doves don't fight."

I pondered the difference between pigeons and doves as Pete spoke. I now wish to apply them to my own observations of certain aspects of church life, including some of the mistakes I have made.

A PIGEON CAN LOOK LIKE A DOVE

My wife, Louise, and I spend most of our holidays in the Florida Keys. Doves and pigeons are both common there. One of my favorite fishing spots is next to a very small island called Dove Key, so named because doves love to nest there. Because of its name, you expect to see doves there, and you assume you are looking at doves when you get fairly close. The name has preconditioned you to see doves. But pigeons are there, too!

When one is preconditioned for a certain manifestation of the Holy Spirit, it is easy to presume the presence of the genuine Holy Spirit when you see that particular manifestation. Take falling down and laughing as an example. Now I happen to believe that God has truly turned up in some places where the phenomena of falling down and laughing have been the authentic results. But when one attends a church where this happens a lot, it's likely that someone could easily fall to the floor after being prayed for and that there could be an entirely natural explanation for it.

Several years ago, because I was sitting on the front

row, I felt compelled to come forward when the preacher asked all church leaders to line up for prayer in the front. I sincerely hoped that God would come down on me and do whatever He pleased. Seventy or eighty men and women were lined up ahead of me for prayer. As the preacher prayed for each person, every single person fell backwards into the arms of the "catcher" waiting next in line. Then the preacher came to me. I stood there like the Statue of Liberty. Nothing happened.

He prayed again, then a third time. Had I closed my eyes and been less conscious of standing straight, I suspect I too would have fallen. I felt sorry for the preacher and wanted to apologize for his embarrassment when I didn't fall. I wanted to—I promise you. But I didn't want to be pushed over by a pigeon, either!

I'm not saying that the Dove did not come down on some, if not all of the other people in that line. But I believe that their expectancy was so high and the preconditioning so powerful that a pigeon may well have done the same thing.

Pigeons may be present whenever God shows up in genuine Holy Spirit power. On one night there may be a most awesome sense of God's power. You may feel it in the worship, in the preaching and in the time of prayer ministry. People may be shedding tears of joy and repentance and laughing and crying. Scores may be converted, and many healed.

You can't wait for the next night. That night the same worship group leads with the same songs and hymns. The same preacher takes his text from God's Word. But God chooses not to show up.

The important issue is this: Will the minister in charge have the integrity not to manipulate the people? Or will he feel that to be successful, that night's meeting must appear to be just like the meeting on the previous night? If he thinks that, it is likely he may practice pigeon religion in order to get the same results.

The genuine Dove is like the wind that blows "wherever it pleases" (John 3:8). If one is truly sensitive to the Spirit, he or she must flow with the Spirit as well. And if one is equally sensitive to His absence, that person will honor God's sovereignty and will not pretend. It takes a lot of courage to yield to the Spirit when He comes in power. It takes equal courage to be unpretentious when He is absent. Both aspects of the Dove can threaten one's comfort zone.

There is nothing like a large crowd to counterfeit the presence of the Dove. A high number of people can create an atmosphere of expectancy. Nothing preconditions a leader or a congregation like a filled church. If there is a lack of discernment and sensitivity to the person of the Spirit, which is needed all the more at such a time, a pigeon could come down on the heads of everyone present, and no one would know the difference. I fear this has happened many times—and to the best of people.

The initial similarity of appearance between a pigeon and the Dove can even produce a "bandwagon" effect—everyone becomes excited and wants to be "in" on what is happening. This can continue for some time. But eventually one wakes up and comes to terms with the sobering possibility that it was all hype. It hurts when you realize you were taken in and that there was a very fleshly explanation for everything that happened.

This can happen at an individual level as well, whether it be through speaking in tongues or through prophetic words of knowledge. If we convince ourselves that God *must* manifest Himself, we will settle for almost anything. It is almost as though one says, "Well, if I can't have the Dove, I'll take a pigeon." But if we believe that Jesus Christ is the same yesterday, today and forever, we ought not to settle for the counterfeit.

A PIGEON WILL EASILY ADJUST TO US

A pigeon can be domesticated, trained and manipulated. A pigeon can be easily controlled and made to conform. Not so a turtledove. Nor can the Spirit of God be easily manipulated or controlled: "The wind blows wherever it pleases. You hear its sound, but you cannot tell where it comes from or where it is going. So it is with everyone born of the Spirit" (John 3:8). True conversion is a sovereign act of God. You cannot make the Holy Dove do anything—except when you make it fly away.

Feeling the need to control the Holy Spirit may be one of the greatest abuses of the Spirit. When we begin to feel we can control the will of the Holy Spirit, pigeon religion has moved in. Yet often we continue trying to convince ourselves that it must be the Dove.

The issue is control. Who's in charge? Some people play with the Holy Spirit as if He has no will of His own. We can fall prey to this when we are praying alone by attempting to do all the talking—thus quenching the Spirit. Or we can read the Bible and do all the thinking. In this way, the Dove does not have a chance to slip in—He is too much of a gentleman in any case.

The same can happen with public leadership. A powerful leader (even a worship leader or preacher) can sometimes control a crowd with his or her gift and personality. The people out there may not have a clue they are being manipulated.

The problem lies in the fact that one's gift is, in a sense, also one's anointing. God shapes each gift and personality for His glory. However, not everything that someone with an anointed gift does is Spirit led. We are under a solemn obligation to follow—not lead—the Holy Spirit. I may have an anointing to teach and preach, but I can get

149

ahead of the Lord as Joseph and Mary did. When I do, pigeon religion takes over because I am in control.

Some years ago I talked with a worship leader about his style of leading worship. He admitted he had a gifting that enabled him to control an audience. He could make them do almost anything—clap, jump, sit or weep. When he did this, the people never knew they had been conditioned for a certain response in much the same way pigeons are trained to perform some behavior. It is an exceedingly rare worship leader who is utterly sensitive to the Dove and does not get ahead of the Lord.

In 1963 I pastored a church in Carlisle, Ohio. I read in the newspaper that a Christian minister (written up in *Time* magazine) who was a leader in the Charismatic Movement was coming to Middletown, Ohio—less than ten miles away. I decided to go to hear him speak. When I met him before the service, he told me he was a Calvinist who spoke in tongues.[1] That interested me. At the end of the service I stayed behind for prayer. I knelt at the altar and prayed, "Lord, if this is from You, let it come; if not, stop it." That is all I said. But I meant it.

The man prayed for me to receive the gift of tongues. But nothing happened. He then asked me to take literally the words, "Make a joyful noise unto the Lord." I wasn't sure what that meant. He said, "Just make a joyful noise." I was feeling a bit strange by this time. "Just make a noise," he continued.

Feeling a bit impatient, I pleaded, "I don't understand."

"Just say 'Ah,'" the man instructed me.

The pressure on me to speak in tongues was now so intense that I burst into a nervous fit of giggles, which the dear brother took to mean that the Holy Spirit had come. He hadn't—I was only laughing nervously. Now I felt manipulated because I hadn't met his expectations.

I was experiencing pigeon religion.

On the other hand, I do believe that some people (whom I know well) have indeed truly received the gift of tongues by being gently led by a godly person who was sensitive to the Spirit. The problem with me was that I probably wasn't ready, and I doubt the Dove was ready, either. I know I was open at first but not at the end. Had the Christian leader been sensitive to the Spirit, the fiasco could have been avoided.

Pigeon religion is man in control. It is manipulative, usurping the place of the Dove. The gracious Spirit is gentle and prudent. Like the meek and lowly Jesus, the Dove is neither intrusive (coming when not invited) nor obtrusive (unpleasantly noticeable). He is self-effacing. When He is invited and accepts the invitation, the result takes man out of the picture.

When the Spirit is present, people want to wait upon the Spirit. They want to worship, and they let the Spirit do the leading. When this happens, it is an unforgettable experience—one worth waiting for.

The Holy Spirit will not be manipulated. The Dove flutters away as soon as one tries to do this, and the pigeon comes in.

PIGEON RELIGION IS TERRITORIAL

A pigeon thinks a certain place belongs to him. Pigeon religion is manifested when one instinctively feels he or she has a "corner" on the anointing. This happens when we take ourselves too seriously. It also happens when we decide we own the franchise on God's enterprise in a particular theological or geological area. As a result, we struggle against someone else "elbowing in" on our calling, area of expertise or following.

This is a party spirit, a rival or competitive spirit. Because we uphold a particular emphasis, we want to be the sole vanguard for the "party line." We expect such a spirit to be present in partisan politics when a political party champions an issue that has been neglected. That political party wants to be the first to stress "their" special issue—whether it be the environment, social justice or lowering taxes. Therefore a politician from that party resents it when a rival party wants to take the same line—even if in a different way. This is often seen when a party, whether known to be on the right or the left, moves toward the center. Politicians are territorial.

However, nothing is more deadly than a rival spirit in the church of God. Take the subject of revival, for example. I think we all generally agree that there is a heart cry for revival today. I doubt there is any evangelical group or church that is not praying for revival—a sovereign outpouring of God's Spirit that will revive the people of God and result in many conversions.

The problem is, we all want it to come to *us*! We all tend to see ourselves as having "borne the burden of the work and the heat of the day" (Matt. 20:12). We resent it if God makes others "equal to us"! We want God to bless *our* efforts, *our* party line, *our* denomination or group. Therefore we tend to dismiss any report of God coming down powerfully on anyone but *us*. We honestly believe it couldn't happen to those who are of a different theological persuasion or ecclesiastical setting.

Not long ago a weekly prayer meeting on the second floor of a civic center in Nairobi, Kenya, centered on revival. A group of a dozen Western missionaries prayed earnestly that God would send revival to Nairobi. At exactly the same time, seven hundred Kenyans were praying noisily and worshiping God—and growing rapidly—in the large auditorium just beneath the group of Western missionaries. The irony is, God was answering the missionaries' prayers! But they could not

bring themselves to recognize revival under their noses—
for the Kenyans below them didn't represent their party
line. Another example of pigeon religion!

None of us have a monopoly on the anointing. Jesus'
disciples wanted to stop someone praying in Jesus' name
"because he is not one of us." (See Luke 9:49–50.) Jesus
stepped in, admonishing, "Do not stop him...for whoever is not against you is for you." This is a reminder
that we should rejoice over—not resent—someone
praying in Jesus' name, even when that person is not a
part of "our" group.

Even Joshua, when he was young and still had a lot to
learn, was unhappy when certain people were prophesying without recognized credentials. "But Moses replied,
'Are you jealous for my sake? I wish that all the LORD's
people were prophets and that the LORD would put his
Spirit on them!'" (Num. 11:29). That is the way God
wants us all to reject pigeon religion and pray for the
restoration of God's honor in the world—not just on our
own small ministries.

Pigeon religion easily creeps into denominational jour-
nals and party line magazines. Each tends, understand-
ably, to uphold the party line. We have our own in-house
magazine at Westminster Chapel. But if I ever allow any
article to attack a servant of Christ—whatever his or her
party line—it will not be under the anointing of the Dove.
"Doves don't fight each other," says my friend Pete. But
pigeons do. Any personal attack upon a fellow believer
is almost certainly not under the leadership of the Spirit
of God. As my old Kentucky friend C. B. Fugett used to
say, even if crudely, "The God in me will not fight the
God in you." This means that the Holy Spirit will not
attack Himself—another person who is sincerely following Christ or a movement that clearly desires to uphold
the honor and name of God.

153

USURPING THE PRIVILEGE THAT
BELONGS ONLY TO THE SPIRIT

The Spirit will do His work—if I don't get in the way. We must not step in where we don't belong or elbow in on the Spirit's territory. For the Spirit to be able to do His work, we must simply be the channel through which He works. If we try to do what He does best, He flutters away.

It can happen in the pulpit. In my forty-five years of preaching, it's happened to me far too many times. It happens often if I preach with a particular person in mind, trying too hard to make sure he or she gets the point. That borders on preaching *at* the people.

There are five preaching positions we can look at:

- Preaching *down* to the people—this patronizes the listener.

- Preaching *up* to the people—this occurs when I am intimidated by the people to whom I preach.

- Preaching *for* the people—this is a form of preaching done for entertainment.

- Preaching *at* the people—in reality, this is cowardice.

- Preaching *to* the people—which is what one is supposed to do.

When I preach at the people I am abusing my privilege and forfeiting the release of the Spirit's power on them. I am taking advantage of the platform God has given me. The people to whom I do this are helpless to make a response to me, and as a result, my preaching becomes the folly of the flesh.

Someone has said that the pulpit is no more the

preacher's own platform than is the communion table. When I conduct the Lord's Supper, I must focus upon Christ's death and all that it provides to the believer. I dare not presume to abuse this responsibility. Nor dare I abuse my responsibility when I preach. The pulpit is the Spirit's platform, and when I get personally involved, I compete with what is His sole prerogative.

When I preach, more often than not I have found that the very people I had hoped would be present because I felt I had a word for them are, in actuality, absent. And should those people *be* present, they are usually the last to apply the word to themselves! But when I forget who is present and how the word might be applied, God will often apply that word powerfully.

People can usually tell if it is truly God who is speaking to them. In fact, it is often counterproductive if they sense the preacher thinks he has a word for them. It is possible to begin in the Spirit and end up in the flesh in our attempts at "doing ministry." Pigeon religion sets in when I get in the way of the sensitive Dove who works—but without competition. As a friend of mine has often said that unlike most of us, the Holy Spirit is the only perfect preacher, the only one who never calls attention to Himself.

ANGER IN THE PRESENCE OF GOD

I've been guilty of expressing anger and resentment about "what *they* did" and "how could they do it?" At times, pigeon religion has followed me right into my quiet time with God. The Dove may be a thousand miles away, but I'll tell myself the Holy Spirit is with me in my rash praying. Mind you, it is better to gripe to the Lord than to take it out on someone else. The psalmist said, "I pour out my complaint before him; before him I tell my trouble" (Ps. 142:2).

It isn't all bad to complain to God like this. The problem

begins when I think the Holy Spirit is egging me on to feel as I do—and I think He is as upset as I am! When my agitation persuades me that God is as angry as I am, I am praying in the flesh. This is sheer pigeon religion. I am taking the low road when I pray for God to punish someone with whom I have a complaint. God may tolerate this kind of prayer, but He isn't being honored in it.

When at last I start praying that God will *bless* my enemy, I can immediately feel God say, "That's better." This is what He wanted all along. This is *always* the will of the Holy Spirit.

We saw earlier that God sometimes teases us to believe the opposite of what He really feels—to test us. God did this with Moses. When the people of Israel were rebellious and not listening to Moses, God made a proposition to him using these words:

> "I have seen these people," the LORD said to Moses, "and they are a stiff-necked people. Now leave me alone so that my anger may burn against them and that I may destroy them. Then I will make you into a great nation."
>
> —EXODUS 32:9–10

I fear that, had I been Moses, I would have said YES! to His offer. There have been times one could wish God would step in and wipe out certain people—for good. But Moses took a different line: NO!

> But Moses sought the favor of the LORD his God. "O LORD," he said, "why should your anger burn against your people, whom you brought out of Egypt with great power and a mighty hand? Why should the Egyptians say, 'It was with evil intent that he brought them out, to kill them in the mountains and to wipe them off the face of the earth'? Turn from your fierce anger; *relent and do not bring disaster on your people.* Remember your

servants Abraham, Isaac and Israel, to whom you swore by your own self: 'I will make your descendants as numerous as the stars in the sky and I will give your descendants all this land I promised them, and it will be their inheritance forever.'" Then the LORD relented and did not bring on his people the disaster he had threatened.

—EXODUS 32:11–14, EMPHASIS ADDED

The prayer Moses prayed was exactly what God hoped he would pray. It shows Moses' true greatness. Greatness is graciousness. Sir Winston Churchill used to say that the price of greatness is responsibility.

It is so easy to get personally and emotionally involved in our own enterprise and forget it is God's work and reputation that matter—not ours. Anger in God's presence is understandable, but it is never right. When the Dove comes down, the result will be our rising above our natural instincts by asking God to bless and forgive our enemies. Anger will disappear, and we will be filled with love and gratitude.

WHEN THE NATURAL CAMOUFLAGES AS THE ANOINTING

In my book *The Anointing: Yesterday, Today, Tomorrow* I wrote about what some of us refer to as "common grace." Calvin calls it "special grace in nature." It refers to the sheer natural ability one may have, which, nonetheless, is a gift of God. These abilities are not a part of regeneration (being born again). It is what enabled Arthur Rubenstein to play the piano. It lay behind Rachmaninov's *Concerto in C Minor* or Albert Einstein's great brain.

A Christian has it, too. *Common grace* is God's goodness to all men and women. When a Christian, especially a church leader, is highly gifted, that person could function admirably without much immediate help from the Holy Spirit. The Christian orators of this world who possess sharp communicative skills must be very cautious with these abilities. I suspect they could carry on before vast audiences without the anointing of the Spirit if they tried—and few, if any, could tell.

These natural abilities are not limited to oratorical powers. A Christian who is gifted in making money could continue to do so without a fervent, private prayer life. One could be a lawyer, physician, nurse or writer and be productive without having to forgive his or her enemies, graciously dignify trials or pay tithes. Those looking on would never know whether the presence of the Dove was powerfully present in that person's private life.

The great danger in this regard is the possibility of self-deception. Because the flow of God's special grace at the level of natural ability seems so real, the individual might think, *God is truly with me. If He wasn't, I would not be so good at what I do.* The momentum of a natural gifting can go a long way. One may carry on toward Galilee and leave Jesus behind and never know the difference. It is hard to reach or teach people like this. They often see little wrong in their lives. Sometimes it takes a tragedy—financial reverse, marriage or family breakdown, serious illness or accident—to get their attention.

WHEN A GIFT OF THE SPIRIT CAMOUFLAGES AS THE ANOINTING

The gifts of the Spirit are "irrevocable" (Rom. 11:29). They are retained regardless of the closeness of one's walk with God. For this reason, the manifestation of such gifts may prevent a person from listening further to God.

King Saul lost his special anointing, but he continued to exercise the gift of prophecy. (See 1 Samuel 16:1; 18:12.) Indeed, on his way to kill David he began prophesying spontaneously (1 Sam. 19:23). Apparently the fact that he was consumed with hatred and jealousy for David did not affect the functioning of that gift of the Spirit one bit.

Paul expressed his concern about this possibility to the Corinthians, who thought that speaking in tongues proved that they were spiritual. "Wrong!" says Paul. In response he wrote 1 Corinthians 12 and 14, pointing out to the Corinthians that love was the "*most* excellent way" (1 Cor. 12:31, emphasis added).

The gift of tongues can be used by a believer despite that person's bitterness and disobedience. It is used by some as evidence that they are perfectly fine in God's sight. This is another example of pigeon religion.

One of the great mysteries of Samson's unusual anointing was that his weakness for women did not appear to diminish his strength at first. It was not until he told his secret to Delilah that he lost it all. Perhaps this helps explain how a Christian can seem to get away with sexual improprieties and carry on with apparent effectiveness. It is as though one flourishes until he or she gets caught! I know many stories that illustrate this point. I don't understand this fact, but such behavior indicates an insensitivity to the Dove before the stark truth is out in the open.

God will eventually hold one accountable for practicing such hypocrisy: "For God will judge the adulterer and all the sexually immoral" (Heb. 13:4). Our Lord demonstrated a lot of patience with sexual sin. (See John 8:1–11.) However, God requires holiness among His people.

> It is God's will that you should be sanctified: that you should avoid sexual immorality; that each of you should learn to control his own body in a way

159

that is holy and honorable...The Lord will punish men for all such sins, as we have already told you and warned you.

—1 THESSALONIANS 4:3–4, 6

Some day it will be payday. Sin will be found out. If you are involved in a relationship that is dishonoring to God, regardless of how your spiritual gift functions, I urge you to break it off. Stop it. Fall on your face before God, confess it and turn from it. God will forgive you (1 John 1:9). The Dove will return as soon as the pigeon is out of the picture.

DON'T SETTLE FOR A SUBSTITUTE

There are some things in the natural that can appear to be a substitute for the purity of the Spirit of God. Avoid these things.

A PLEASANT PERSONALITY MAY LOOK LIKE THE FRUIT OF THE SPIRIT.

There are people who are just simply nice. They are sweet, friendly and cheerful. They are the type of person you want to be around all the time. However, sometimes an aspect of God's common grace is substituting for the Spirit's manifestation. At times their pleasant personalities can put Christians who have been saved for years to shame. But their pleasantness may have nothing whatever to do with the fruit of the Spirit. In actuality, they acted the same way before they were converted.

It can be difficult to convince people like this of their own need to exhibit the fruit of the Spirit. But sooner or later their self-righteousness will surface if they haven't been convicted of sin. If you recognize this problem in yourself, I urge you to do two things:

ꭣ Thank God for your pleasing temperament.

160

ॐ Pray harder than ever to be sensitive to sin
  and to the Spirit.

EMOTIONAL MATURITY CAN LOOK LIKE
SPIRITUAL MATURITY.

Some people grow up faster than others, and some
develop spiritually more quickly than others. There
are many explanations for this. If one has developed
emotionally in a manner that shows fewer psychologi-
cal problems, it should not be surprising that he or she
appears spiritually mature as well. A person like this may
or may not be strong in private prayer, worship and Bible
reading, but will nonetheless appear level-headed and
responsible compared to a neurotic Christian who prays
all the time!

Regeneration and sanctification do not necessarily
eradicate damaged emotions that come from abuse or
neglect as one was growing up. For this reason a Christian who had severely damaged emotions as a child may
struggle in areas that a relatively unspiritual person finds
easy. The latter may appear to be more godly, when this
may not really be the case. Matthew warns us, "Do not
judge, or you too will be judged" (Matt. 7:1).

For some people, then, the appearance of the Dove
may not be the explanation for their apparent maturity.
Yet these same people are often the ones who get voted
into positions of church leadership and who go into full-
time ministry.

They are not unlike King Saul—they have the *influence* but not necessarily the *anointing*. Pigeon religion
is widespread in the church. As I mentioned earlier, a
recent poll showed that the average church leader spends
only *four minutes a day* in quiet time.

The problem becomes even more complicated when
ordinary Christians—beset with emotional difficulties

161

but nonetheless consumed with a love for God and His Word—feel that their church leaders aren't very spiritual.

CULTURAL AND INTELLECTUAL TASTES CAN APPEAR TO BE THEOLOGICAL MATURITY.

Some people have a head start when it comes to upbringing. They are brought up with poise, elegance and a certain aptitude for intellectual things. They go to the better schools. They have a cerebral framework that some do not have.

When people like this become Christians, they may take to Pauline theology like a cat chasing a mouse. Does this mean they are more spiritual? Possibly, but not necessarily. There could be a natural explanation.

People who are very theologically minded are not necessarily more interested in the things of the Spirit. They often think it is far more important to articulate the implications of justification by faith alone than to be personally filled with the Spirit.

162

At the other end of the spectrum are people who are more interested in things of the Spirit than they are in the intricacies of theological orthodoxy. But these people are not necessarily more spiritual. Because they often lack theological training, these people may just be drawn more naturally to experiential knowledge than to doctrine.

We must resist the temptation to be judgmental about things that are opposed to our own interest levels. Often what appeals to a believer can be explained in natural terms rather than by Holy Spirit-motivated explanation.

In a word: Pigeon religion may emerge in either case.

I have one final word on the subject of pigeon religion. What looks like a pigeon may actually be a dove! What we are tempted to identify as pigeon religion may turn out to be God at work! I talked earlier about Dove Key, Florida, where doves nest by the thousands. But there is also a small island called Pigeon Key—located just under the seven-mile bridge between Marathon and Key West, Florida. No doubt there are times when a dove nests there also, just as pigeons try to nest on Dove Key.

We are as capable of following pigeon religion as we are of following the Holy Dove. Simon Peter was being led by the Dove when he said to Jesus, "You are the Christ, the Son of the living God" (Matt. 16:16). Jesus told Peter that Peter's confession of Christ as the Son of God had not been revealed to him "by man, but by my Father in heaven" (v. 17). Yet just a few verses later, "Jesus turned and said to Peter, 'Get behind me, Satan! You are a stumbling block to me; you do not have in mind the things of God, but the things of men'" (v. 23).

I have had to back off from a strong public stand against a person or group that I felt was practicing pigeon religion more often than I care to admit. I have seen that which I have called a *pigeon* being owned by God as His *Dove*. Moreover, God can see a rough diamond—a stone nobody would initially suspect as real—and use him or her while the rest of us smugly uphold our own interests. The late Rolfe Barnard used to say, "One day somebody is going to come along, pick up the Bible and believe it— and put the rest of us to shame."

There is surely nothing worse than for God to reveal His glory and we miss it. It would have been impossible to convince the ancient Pharisees, Sadducees and teachers of the Law that the Messiah could show up and they not recognize Him. But it happened! An ever-increasing sensitivity to the Dove is our best guarantee against the discovery that He is missing from our lives.

CHAPTER NINE

The Road Back

They went back to Jerusalem to look for him.

—Luke 2:45

When we sense the anointing has been lifted from our lives, the most natural thing in the world is to return to our comfort zones. When Joseph and Mary realized that Jesus was missing, the first place they sought Him was among relatives and friends (Luke 2:44). Where else? Why look elsewhere? What other place would they have thought of? What other frame of reference would they know about?

But Joseph and Mary did not find Him where they expected to find Him. He simply wasn't there. To find Him, they had to go back to the place where they lost Him.

What, then, are you and I to do once we come to terms with the loss of our anointing? In this chapter we will examine the way back. The journey back to Jerusalem, where we find the presence of Jesus, involves passing through some important stages.

REPENTANCE

The word *repentance* comes from the Greek word *metanoia*, which means literally "change of mind." Joseph and Mary would not have thought a change of mind was necessary in their relationship with Jesus. They thought He was with them. They were wrong. They had to admit they were wrong.

In part, repentance means admitting, "I was wrong." Unfortunately, we never come to the place of saying "I was wrong" until we are forced to do so. Joseph and Mary headed back to Jerusalem only because they could not find Jesus. The natural inclination in all of us is to defend where we are and why. Unless we are forced out of our comfort zone we will stay in it.

Joseph and Mary had no choice. Like it or not, they were wrong to think that Jesus was with them. When they made a U-turn, they were saying that they had been wrong in supposing Jesus to have been in their company. It took irrefutable evidence that He was nowhere near to persuade them to turn back. When they couldn't find Him, they made the U-turn. We are all like that.

God has to get our attention before we will repent. The last thing on earth we want to do is admit to being wrong. God gets our attention by making us see what we have lost. As long as we can feel we haven't really lost His special presence, we are going to carry on.

Our natural giftings—even our supernatural gifts—will often mask as the anointing. In a sense, such a gift *is* the anointing. After all, our natural ability has a close connection to the divine calling upon our lives. A special gift of the Spirit is—in some sense—an anointing.

There are two ways by which one is called to repentance.

1. *You admit God's special presence is gone.* Rather than continue as though nothing happened, you repent.

2. *You get caught—exposed.* Someone discovers the truth. Someone "spills the beans." Public shame results. Although this may happen to a believer, I suspect that exposure was necessary at the beginning. Almost certainly, God was trying to get that person to the truth all along.

If people do not admit that God's special presence is gone and repent, God resorts to the second plan—public exposure. When one is forced to repent because of public exposure, the depth of the repentance remains an open question. But one must not be too quick to question the validity of a repentance due to getting caught in error. Apparently King David had no plans to repent until the prophet Nathan confronted him. Yet David's repentance was genuine (2 Sam. 12:13). God can use open exposure and confrontation to get a person's attention.

As for Joseph and Mary, they were certainly hemmed in. All the people traveling with them knew the truth: Jesus wasn't with them. It wasn't merely an inward feeling that Jesus was not with them. It was obvious to everyone who had been on the journey with them. It must have been somewhat embarrassing.

To be granted repentance is a gracious mercy of God. As the Word teaches us, we are "changed...from glory to glory" as a result of repentance (2 Cor. 3:18, KJV). When we discover new ways to please God...when a renewed measure of His presence reveals our sin and leads to our forgiveness and greater ability to do God's will…we have received insight. The worst thing that can happen to a man or woman is to become stone deaf to the Holy Spirit, losing all sensitivity to His voice. If we do, we will be unable to be renewed through His call to repentance. (See Hebrews 6:6.)

We should be exceedingly grateful that God succeeds in getting our attention and motivating us to make a one-hundred-eighty-degree turn in our lives. We should take any rebuke, discipline or chastening with both hands! "Because the Lord disciplines those he loves, and he punishes everyone he accepts as a son" (Heb. 12:6). The word *discipline*, or *chasten* (KJV), comes from a Greek word that means "enforced learning." Enforced learning takes place when we have virtually no choice but to take God's will on board. It demonstrates not only God's love for us, but also the fact that God isn't finished with us yet. Never forget this: When God chastens us, it means we have a future and that the best is yet to come!

The way back to Jerusalem is the way of repentance. It is admitting that we have lost the special presence of God and have been wrong in our thinking and presumption.

SEEKING GOD'S FACE

Joseph and Mary went back to Jerusalem "to look for *him*" (Luke 2:45, emphasis added). They were looking for a person. They were looking for someone they would recognize. No one else would do. No comfort zone would do; no holy place would suffice. They wanted to find *Him*.

> I will get up now and go about the city,
>> through its streets and squares;
> I will search for the one my heart loves.

So I looked for him but did not find him.

—SONG OF SOLOMON 3:2

One thing I ask of the LORD,
  this is what I seek:
that I may dwell in the house of the LORD
  all the days of my life,
to gaze upon the beauty of the LORD
  and to seek him in his temple.

—PSALM 27:4

One reason God hides His face is because He wants us to seek Him—to go looking for Him. By seeing what our reaction is when He hides His face, He can test our earnestness to seek Him.

Will we recognize the difference between the flow of our natural giftings and the flow of God's special presence? Will we notice the difference between those endowments that are bestowed via common grace and the anointing that has its origin in the radiance of His face? Will we discern the difference between a gift of the Spirit—which is irrevocable—and the intimacy that kindles holy fire?

Are we sensitive to the Dove? Will the counterfeit do? Never! It is only a matter of time until we notice what we have lost when Jesus stays behind. When we see our loss, we must seek His face in repentance. The U-turn back to seeking Him is not enough. It's not enough merely to admit we've been wrong. That is only the beginning.

We must go looking for Jesus. It will take us outside our comfort zones to places we've never been. It wasn't enough for Joseph and Mary to go to Jerusalem. Once there, they still had to find *Him*. Obviously, He wasn't where they thought He would be, for they took three days to find Him. Remember that you can step out of a flowing stream, but you can never step back in at the same place. The flow moves on.

Familiar theology can be a very common comfort zone. So too can a familiar liturgy, clichés or style of worship. We may begin to look for Christ in our comfort zones, but what if He isn't there? Will we admit to this, too?

Seeking the face of the Lord is to settle for nothing but Him. We must seek Him until we find Him. It may require examining teaching we had previously dismissed out of hand. It may mean associating with people we once said we'd have nothing to do with. It may be singing choruses we previously felt were meaningless to us.

Those who had concentrated only on the things of the Spirit may have to go seeking God's Word with a greater thirst than before. Those who were at home with the Word and the finer points of theology may have to submit to a ministry of prayer carried out by people they had once sneered at. Traditionalists may have to sing contemporary songs. Contemporary-style worshipers may have to seek God by singing two-hundred-year-old hymns. Once God has succeeded in getting our attention, we will have to repent and seek God's face without giving up until we find Him. The journey back may require a lot of humbling, sheer embarrassment.

Many years ago Louise developed a condition in her jaw that barely allowed her to open her mouth. A doctor said she required fairly major surgery. We never knew what caused it. But she reached the place where she could hardly chew and could only drink liquid soups without pain.

During this time I met a man who had founded a rescue mission for homeless people. He took in old furniture, fixed it and sold it in order to support his mission. He lived by faith and hard work. He was uneducated, and he had a rather weird theology. I was so impressed with him that I asked him to come to our home for supper. The evening was thrilling as he told us of remarkable answers to prayer. He proceeded to leave about eleven o'clock. As he headed for the door, I told him about Louise's jaw. Without asking for her permission, he simply put down his briefcase, placed his hand on her jaw and said, "In Jesus' name, be healed!" Then he looked at her and said, "Now open your jaw." She did! She was healed on the spot. It seemed no big deal to him. He picked up his briefcase and went home.

I learned a lesson that night. God can place an unusual anointing on someone with whose theology I am rather uncomfortable. Through the years, I have learned that God is often found where we have no intention of looking. But when we are desperate, all that can change.

Jephthah was one of the lesser-known people in the Bible. (See Judges 11.) All of Israel had rejected him. But the time came when they were so desperate that they turned to him. He saved the day and is given mention in Hebrews 11:32. But he was the last person they wanted to turn to for help. God has a way of bringing all our options down to one—the last option we wanted! It is part of God's sense of humor!

Seeking God's face means settling for nothing but the special presence of God—and not stopping until you know you have found Him wherever He is.

NOT GIVING UP

"After three days they found him" (Luke 2:46). It took one day to lose Jesus, and three days to find Him. It is easier to lose the anointing than it is to get it back. But if we truly want to recover His presence in our lives, it can happen. God does not tease us, dangling a carrot to demoralize us.

Do not be deceived: God cannot be mocked. A man

reaps what he sows. The one who sows to please his
sinful nature, from that nature will reap destruction;
the one who sows to please the Spirit, from the Spirit
will reap eternal life. Let us not become weary in doing
good, for at the proper time we will reap a harvest if we
do not give up.

—Galatians 6:7–9

Three days is a relatively short period of time in which
to seek the Lord. But if we are to see the account of Joseph
and Mary as a parallel, it suggests that it could take three
times as long to reexperience the special presence of God
as it takes to lose it. We must be prepared to take as much
time as necessary to get back what we lost. Any effort or
any amount of time is worth it.

My own return to Jerusalem has included a great deal
of praying, fasting, tithing and occasions of being willing to "lose face." I do not know what you may have to
do to regain God's presence if you have experienced the
withdrawal of the Dove. But I can share some of what I
have had to do.

DIGNIFY THE TRIAL.

During the autumn of 1979 I had planned to preach
through the Book of James. But I was haunted by the
opening exhortation: "Consider it pure joy, my brothers, whenever you face trials of many kinds" (James 1:2).
That verse didn't square with my penchant for being the
world's greatest complainer! Something big needed to
happen to me, but God taught the lesson to me through
a small thing, which is often His way.

I remember it as though it were yesterday. I was in
Kissimmee, Florida, near Disney World. The previous
year I had taken the family to Disney World, and they
wanted to go back. I was quite ready to agree—mainly
because I would be able to return to a pizza shop in Kis-

172

simmee where, the previous year, I had eaten the most succulent, delicious pizza of my life! So on the day we checked into our motel in Kissimmee, we headed for the pizza parlor. Each of us ordered a pizza to suit our own taste. I ordered the "works"—everything available, including anchovies.

Somehow the chef forgot our order, and forty-five minutes later I let him know in a most articulate manner that I was not happy. It was his first day at work. Finally he called us to the counter and handed us our pizzas. I paid without a smile.

Just before we left to return to our motel, it started raining. Now when it rains in Florida, it rains! Although the motel was less than a mile away, by the time we drove up next to our room there was almost a foot of water. Louise and the kids took their pizzas and made a run for it. I opened my door, stepped in a foot of water and opened the back door to get my pizza. The rain poured down on that brown paper bag with my pizza, and out came everything—anchovies, peppers, mushrooms, sausages, pepperoni—straight into a puddle of water. I reported my grievous loss to my family, each family member busily digging into their pizzas, and headed back to the pizza parlor.

Something wonderful happened. I don't understand it; I can only say that God was gracious. As I drove to the restaurant, I thought of James 1:2: "Consider it pure joy, my brothers, whenever you face trials of many kinds." *Either this verse is true, or it isn't*, I thought. I made a decision then and there to dignify that little trial (although it seemed big at the time). I confessed my anger to God and promised I would, from then on, accept the smallest trial as a gift from Him. An old hymn says it this way:

Ev'ry joy or trial falleth from above,

173

> Trac'd upon our dial by the Sun of Love;
> We may trust Him fully all for us to do;
> They who trust Him wholly find Him wholly true.[1]

Suddenly the most wonderful peace came over me, the greatest I had experienced since October 31, 1955. I went to that chef on bended knee and told him what had happened. I said that I would gladly wait for him to do another pizza for me. He didn't even charge me! I will never forget those moments. The next day—all day long—at Disney World I was aglow with a great measure of renewal of the Spirit.

This incident taught me that we must adjust to the Dove in the smallest, though very difficult, episodes of life. To keep the Dove *remaining* is to adjust day and night to every relationship and circumstance.

FORGIVE TOTALLY.

We must not forget what Paul said:

> Get rid of all bitterness, rage and anger, brawling and slander, along with every form of malice. Be kind and compassionate to one another, forgiving each other, just as in Christ God forgave you.
>
> —EPHESIANS 4:31–32, EMPHASIS ADDED

The idea of forgiving others was—to me—head knowledge, I must admit. I also thought that in *my* case of being hurt and maligned, God not only understood, but He also waived the rules. Wrong. In my darkest hour, my old friend Joseph Tson said to me, "R. T., you must *totally forgive* those who hurt you. Until you totally forgive them, you will be in chains."[2]

Forgiving people who had hurt me was the hardest thing I've ever had to do. But the benefits so outweighed my carnal wish that my enemies would get what they deserved that I was never to be the same again. Talk about peace! It began to come back in waves as I prayed for their forgiveness. I actually prayed that they would get away with their sin! After all, the Lord reminded me that I had gotten away with a lot! When I remembered what I had been forgiven of, forgiving others became progressively easier.

WALK IN THE LIGHT.

> But if we walk in the light, as he is in the light, we have fellowship with one another, and the blood of Jesus, his Son, purifies us from all sin.
>
> —1 JOHN 1:7

I have had to make a number of crucial decisions over the past twenty years that led to a greater anointing than I have had before.[3] I have learned to walk in the light, to focus on Jesus and to maintain the awareness of the gentle Holy Spirit as much as possible. I have a long way to go, and I learn new lessons all the time. But I have been sobered by one essential factor: God doesn't bend the principles of the ungrieved Spirit for me. In a word: The Dove does not adjust to me; I have to adjust to Him.

In addition to Paul's affirmation that "God cannot be mocked" (Gal. 6:7), at least twice God put it like this:

> But if from there you seek the LORD your God, you will find him if you look for him with all your heart and with all your soul.
>
> —DEUTERONOMY 4:29

> You will seek me and find me when you seek me with all your heart.
>
> —JEREMIAH 29:13

This means heeding any warnings, any "new" lights in which to walk and any promises the Lord has given us. Whatever we know already that grieves the Spirit must be set aside categorically if we want a renewal of His special presence. Being prayed for by those who have a ministry of prayer and laying on hands will do no harm, but whatever renewal comes from the laying on of hands will wane rather quickly if you do not develop a sensitivity to the Spirit on your own.

Experience God's anointing by learning what makes the Dove feel at home with you. Get all the prayer ministry you can. Sit under the best teaching and preaching you can find. Worship with God's people all you can. But at the end of the day, the anointing that characterizes the Dove is tied to what you are as a person—day and night, at home or at work, with friends and with family, at church or in solitude with Jesus. This is the forgotten anointing.

LEARN TO RECOGNIZE WHAT YOU HAVEN'T SEEN BEFORE.

> After three days they found him in the temple courts, sitting among the teachers, listening to them and asking them questions.
>
> —LUKE 2:46

Mary and Joseph encountered a Jesus they hardly knew! Why? When we are away from the Lord, He moves on. By the time we catch up with Him, He is not the same—to us. He continues to work. But because we have not been in on the work He is doing, we have to make new adjustments to what He is doing at the time we rediscover Him.

Many people who oppose what God is doing—in any generation—are not as close to the Lord as they thought. If they were, they would not be so slow to recognize Him. It is when we move on without Him—while He continues to manifest His glory elsewhere—that our discernment becomes warped. Someone has said, "All is yellow to the jaundiced eye." Our sight of the Lord

176

is often fixed in one direction—the way we knew Him when we last felt Him. But if we move on, and He is at work elsewhere, we must be prepared to bow to Him wherever He is working and whatever He is doing.

Joseph and Mary found Jesus "in the temple courts." That is the last place they looked for Jesus. I don't know where Joseph and Mary looked first. I only know this is the last place they looked. Had they come there first, they could have been spared the anguish of their three-day search.

The Lord is to be found in surprising places. God loves to surprise and astonish. But it soon becomes clear that there is nothing unreasonable in the manner and places He chooses to show Himself.

Jesus was "sitting among the teachers." Perhaps Joseph and Mary were a little hurt that He would do this without them. What an amazing sight to behold—their son sitting among the teachers. No doubt they felt left out; they would have wanted to have been informed that He would be there.

177

From time to time, especially when I see a true servant of Christ accomplish something unusual that I hadn't experienced, or hear that person speak with depths of insight I haven't come up with first, I have to question whether I feel anger toward the Lord or gratitude that I have been able to see His sovereign hand at work. If I am angry (as Mary was), I betray how far I have moved ahead of the Lord. If I feel gratitude, I show I am walking in the Spirit—which is a wonderful place to be. I can rejoice in what God is doing apart from me—for after all, it is His glory I want! I have no right to resent what He is pleased to do, wherever it is or with whom. But if I rejoice in it, it is very likely that I will please the Lord.

As Jesus sat with the teachers in the temple, He was "listening to them and asking them questions." Does it surprise us to whom the Lord listens? Do we fancy He only listens to us and to those who hold our points of view?

God's elect are scattered all over the globe. They are made up of every tribe, people, tongue and nation. This includes all cultures, many of whom have unusual ways of worshiping Christ. It does not mean that I must agree with them. It does not necessarily mean the Lord agrees with them. But He listens to them. He listens to my enemies! He loves them, too. When He asks them questions, we don't know their response. But He may well be in communication with them. I should rejoice at any interaction between the Lord and those with whom I may not have close contact.

DON'T BE SURPRISED AT THE EFFECT THE LORD HAS ON OTHERS.

> Everyone who heard him was *amazed* at his understanding and his answers.
>
> —LUKE 2:47, EMPHASIS ADDED

178

While He continues to work without us, He dazzles people we never met. We should rejoice that this is happening. It is to the everlasting credit of the Jews who initially opposed Paul and Barnabas that they were "very glad" once they realized Gentiles had been truly converted. (See Acts 15:3.)

Those who heard Jesus in the temple were "amazed." Jesus always does this. He amazes. He did it without Joseph and Mary. He does it all the time without you and me. When those outside our circles of influence are amazed at Jesus, we should be very glad.

They were amazed at his "understanding and answers." These teachers in the temple courts were not prepared for what they heard. Jesus had a grasp of the things of God that moved them to the core of their beings. You can be sure they needed everything Jesus said. We do not pick up a hint of rejection, only amazement.

We should be thrilled over any report of revival in any part of the world. Yet it is easier to rejoice in a movement of the Spirit in the Third World than across town. If I can praise God for what He is doing in Brazil or India, can I praise God for His blessing on the church across the street from my church—especially if I'm not seeing the same blessing at Westminster Chapel at the moment? Can you praise Him for His blessing in the churches in your community?

What Joseph and Mary saw was right before their eyes. And it was their son at the center of it all! They could not say, "That's not really God," as you and I may want to do if we see something outside our comfort zone. They could not deny that they finally found Jesus. But they only focused on themselves, asking Jesus, "Why have you treated us like this?" (Luke 2:48).

That is about as insensitive as one can get. It goes to show that, though having been previously so close to Jesus, they had become very out of focus in their perception of Him.

It can happen to us. The road back to the anointing must find us thrilled that we ever found our Lord again! We must accept Him as He is and be glad for anything He is doing—wherever it is.

CHAPTER TEN

The Return to the Anointing

When his parents saw him, they were astonished.

—LUKE 2:48

O nce we discover we have moved on without the Lord—and apparently lost a measure of the anointing—our consuming passion is to recover what we once enjoyed. Nothing else really matters when you come to terms with the fact that things are not as they were.

Why must it take so long to return to the anointing? Must it always be true that it is easier to lose the anointing than it is to get it back? Why can't we just apply 1 John 1:9 ("If we confess our sins, he is faithful and just and will forgive us our sins and purify us from all unrighteousness") and be done with it? Won't God instantly forgive once we see that we have erred in moving ahead without Jesus?

Yes. But if that is so, will the anointing not return at once without our having to return to it? Yes, it will should God be pleased to grant it immediately. Sometimes He does. Not all of my own experiences of grieving the Spirit are met with a long period of waiting and agony. Many times the Spirit's anointing returns in moments. In fact, *most* of the time that is what happens.

There are degrees to which we all move ahead without Jesus. There are little ways and big ways by which we forfeit the sense of God's special presence. We can do it by the unguarded comment or by carelessness in small matters such as unimportant decisions. I've done it by getting in the flesh in my preaching. When I come down from the pulpit and realize I said something that was unwarranted, I confess it to God and learn from my mistake. I've had to fulfill invitations that I should not have accepted—in order to learn from my haste.

God is not looking over our shoulders with a magnifying glass to see what He can find that is wrong with us. For one thing He doesn't need a magnifying glass—all things are "uncovered and laid bare" before His eyes (Heb. 4:13). He knows our frame and remembers that we are dust (Ps. 103:14). When we grieve the Spirit in smaller matters, it is true that the Dove distances Himself for a moment. He does us no favor not to do so. But He graciously comes alongside and shows us our folly so that we can confess it and get on with things.

It is important that we learn to recognize the small ways in which we move ahead with the Lord. We need to break these habitual "sprints" away from the Dove in the less important areas in our lives.

But must God hide His face from us for a great length of time when we have erred in a more serious manner? Not necessarily. It may well depend upon our own reaction to His having "stayed behind." In the case of Joseph and Mary, their reaction was anger. As soon as they discovered Jesus' absence, out of their hearts arose the demand: "How dare He do this to us?" Those were the words with which they greeted Him when they found Him in the temple (Luke 2:48). Sometimes it takes a while to return to the anointing because there are some things or attitudes within ourselves that need sorting out.

Take the case of sexual immorality, for example. This sin brings disgrace upon the honor of God's name like no other kind of sin. A greater measure of discipline may be necessary to overcome it. How one reacts to the need of discipline is a factor. There are two possible reactions to "getting caught."

1. *Be sorry at once and avoid becoming defensive.* This was David's reaction when the prophet Nathan confronted him (2 Sam. 12:13). David immediately sought the Lord, wrote Psalm 51 and was given assurance that he would be used again. "Then I will teach transgressors your ways, and sinners will turn back to you" (Ps. 51:13).

2. *Respond with resentment and defensiveness.* Some dig in their heels and resent those who "blew the whistle." People like that are probably going to have to wait a long, long time before they can be restored. They should not blame God if this takes time.

There are incremental degrees by which we move along without Jesus. If you have moved a great distance away from the presence of God, do these things:

~ Admit it.

183

- ❧ Don't be defensive.

- ❧ Turn the matter over to God.

- ❧ Seek His face with all your heart.

Regardless of how much distance there is between you and God, He will meet you where you are—no matter how old you are or how deeply you grieved the Lord! God is a gracious God, and He will begin at once to cause all things to work together for good (Rom. 8:28). This is His promise!

For most of us, the question is, Do we ever truly recover exactly what we lost? I believe the honest answer is both yes and no. Let me explain.

We are never fully prepared for the anxiety that accompanies our journey "back to Jerusalem" or for the sobering discovery of what the return to the anointing entails. The journey back is fraught with anxiety and the fear we might not find what we lost. The three days of looking for Jesus must have seemed like an eternity to Joseph and Mary.

We are also never fully prepared for the way the anointing manifests itself once we find that for which we are looking. Joseph and Mary were "astonished" when they saw Jesus. Was it the same Jesus? Once again the answer is both yes and no. It was Jesus all right. There was no doubt it was He. But in another sense, He was not the Jesus they knew! Never before had they seen Him like this.

They should have been relieved and thankful, but instead they were not altogether happy. Immediately Mary questioned Him. "Son, why have you treated us like this? Your father and I have been anxiously searching for you" (Luke 2:48). Although He was the same Jesus they had known before Jerusalem, because He responded to them differently than they had thought He would, He seemed like a different Jesus to them. And so in a sense He was.

When we find our way back to Jesus, the anointing to which we must return is virtually a *new* anointing. It is new because when we find it again, we must adjust to where it is and how it is manifesting now. Adjusting to the Dove is a lifelong process of agony and surprise.

Some of us take longer in our return *to* the anointing because the whole time we are looking for the return *of* the anointing. We all are prone to say, "The old wine is better."

> And no one after drinking old wine wants the new, for he says, "The old is better."
>
> —Luke 5:39

Each of us tends to begin trying to recover the anointing in our most familiar spot—our comfort zone. But nearly always we do not discover the new anointing until we step outside our comfort zone. God is saying to us, "See, I am doing a new thing!" (Isa. 43:19).

One of the reasons God stays behind and allows us to move on without Him is that we will be forced to see the new and different ways He chooses to manifest His glory. Our first reaction is often the same as that of Mary and Joseph when they finally found Jesus—they were astonished. They wanted the Jesus they knew and were comfortable with. But they were never to have Him exactly like that again.

God's Word advises us:

> Do not say, "Why were the old days better than these?"
> For it is not wise to ask such questions.
>
> —Ecclesiastes 7:10

When Mary Magdalene fell at Jesus' feet and held to

Him, Jesus said, "Do not hold on to me, for I have not yet returned to the Father. Go instead to my brothers and tell them, 'I am returning to my Father and your Father, to my God and your God'" (John 20:17). As gently as He could, He was telling her, "Nothing will be the same again." Mary was beginning the difficult transition from the level of nature, the basic way by which she recognized Jesus, to the level of the Spirit, the new way by which she would have to get accustomed to recognizing Him.

The Christian life is a continual series of events that lead us out of our comfort zones. These repeated transitions take us from the natural level to that of the Spirit. The irony is that even the new level of the Spirit will eventually become another comfort zone to us. It too will have to be left behind in some sense.

Paul Cain recommends that we first erect "no camping allowed" signs at each level of the Spirit to which we move. That will keep us from breaking out of the old mold (no small breakthrough at the time), but then wanting to stay put at the next level. By doing so, the pioneer becomes a settler—something to which we have not been called. We are called to follow the stigma of the Spirit until the day we die, or until the coming of the Lord Jesus. Jesus' disciples were never allowed to "camp."

It was no small thing for the disciples to leave their nets to walk with Jesus. But that was only the beginning. One stigma after another followed. Then came the biggest transition yet. Jesus said, "I am going away" (John 16:7).

> And I will ask the Father, and he will give you another Counselor to be with you forever.
>
> —JOHN 14:16

Leaving their old jobs had been a pivotal experience for the disciples when they began their walk with Jesus. But eventually it had become a settled-in habit. When Jesus told them of His departure, He knew that more battles were on the way. Jesus tried to get the disciples to understand that soon He would be crucified. But they let that message go in one ear and out the other.

Therefore, when He died they were devastated. Then came His resurrection—which thrilled them. During the forty days after His resurrection, Jesus turned up and then disappeared repeatedly—further preparation for the coming of the Spirit. But even after the coming of the Spirit there would be more challenges. Each challenge would catapult them from one comfort zone to a new level of offense.

We will be allowed to become settlers in heaven. Until then we must continue to adjust to the Dove and the surprising and unpredictable ways God challenges our faith. This process is called being changed from "glory to glory" (2 Cor. 3:18, KJV).

If we have lost the anointing—to whatever degree—we must prepare ourselves for the unexpected ways in which God will be found. Like it or not, we can't go back.

PRINCIPLES OF ADJUSTMENT

The principles that I have outlined in this book can be illustrated through the central story of this book. With what did Joseph and Mary have to come to terms? What adjustments did they have to make before returning to Galilee with the Son of God?

GOD MAY WORK WITHOUT OUR INPUT.

Our natural tendency is to expect that we must always be "in the know" about the things of God. This "overfamiliarity" with God often characterizes people who spend a lot of time with Him. We need to check ourselves in this area again and again. God lets us know what we need to know—and keeps from us what He knows would not be good for us to know.

When we get to know God in some depth, we can want some control in the ways He works. We feel as though we have an "in" with God, and before we know it, we think we have some claim on Him. We expect to be informed by Him of every move He makes—and we expect to know it before anyone else has been told.

Joseph and Mary discovered that God was up to something without them—and were upset when they found Jesus. They felt let down. I have felt that way again and again. I may know abstractly that God is "wholly other," as the theologians say (which means He is utterly different in Himself than all His creation). But to see Him manifest Himself in a way *other* than what I have known often makes me think, *This can't be the God I know.*

But it certainly can be God. He is wholly other and entirely sovereign, and He has the right to move in any direction without telling those who may think they are closest to Him.

GOD WILL DO NEW AND DIFFERENT THINGS.

As a twelve-year-old, Jesus sat in the temple courts holding His own with the mature teachers of the Law. He *sat*—the position of a rabbi rather than that of a child— and dazzled the experts, an unprecedented occasion.

It would be difficult to find a biblical mandate or example to validate what Jesus was doing. There simply was no established precedent, tradition or verse in the Old Testament that would put Joseph and Mary at ease. Demanding biblical precedent is a common defense mechanism that many of us use when we wish to reject a particular manifestation of the Spirit. Jonathan Edwards wrote *Religious Affections* because he faced charges that what was happening in his day had no biblical precedent.

In truth, part of the stigma of the presence of God is the *continuation* of God's surprises—from the shock of the cross to the bewilderment of God's latest way of offending us. Hebrews 11 is our precedent—none of the "heroes" described were allowed to repeat the exact manner of obedience that preceded them. Hebrews 11 is, in a sense, still being written by us!

This is a pattern that can be found throughout church history. Those who often thought they were "closest" to God are the very people who became the most astonished at what God was doing. At times these people used their astonishment as a reason to opt out of a situation with a good conscience. It was precisely this fact that caused the chief priests to feel no guilt about crucifying Jesus. Isaiah saw it coming: "We considered him stricken by God, smitten by him" (Isa. 53:4).

At times, God Himself allows a convenient way out for those who hope they don't have to embrace the latest movement of the Spirit. Sometimes someone will say, "Is this not Jesus, the son of Joseph, whose father and mother we know?" (John 6:42), and feel perfectly justified by rejecting Him. Others will find some respectable rationale for staying in their comfort zones. We all have the capacity for avoiding what is unpleasant and feeling good about it.

But none of this takes God by surprise. As the psalmist put it, "If I were hungry I would not tell you" (Ps. 50:12). At times, it would seem that the Holy Spirit is too much of a gentleman to intrude into our fears and biases.

Joseph and Mary were hemmed in and knew this was indeed their son—even if He was a somewhat different Jesus from the one to whom they had been accustomed. All who know what it is to be boxed into a corner like that

189

should feel singularly blessed. I know what it is to be *forced* to see the truth of what I hoped wasn't true—and have to back-pedal. It is painfully embarrassing, but a sign of God's magnanimous mercy. He didn't have to show me the truth in the first place.

MOVE TOWARD THE ANOINTING—DON'T WAIT
FOR IT TO COME TO YOU.

Going to Jerusalem wasn't enough—Joseph and Mary still had to find Jesus. Presumably it took a day merely to get back to Jerusalem, but Jesus had apparently moved to another spot. Finding Jesus took another two days, which meant a total of three days. He didn't come to them; they had to go to Him. They could not give up until they found Him.

When the Toronto phenomenon was at its height, many of us wondered, "Why do people have to go to Toronto to experience this blessing? Or to Holy Trinity Brompton in England?" When someone asked me that question I answered, "And what if we *do* have to go to one of those places? Will we do it?"

You may not have lost your anointing at Toronto, but you *may* have to go there—or to wherever God is powerfully at work—to find God's special presence once again. Would you be willing to do that? If that is where God is at work, will you and I have the humility and integrity to go there, and be utterly open to rediscover God's special presence?

You may say, "God can meet with me in the privacy of my own place of prayer." No doubt He can. But it is my experience that God tests me to the hilt—to see how much I want Him—by not coming to me in power until I seek Him with all my heart, wherever He may be at work. When the leper Naaman was told to seek out Elisha the prophet, he might have said, "Let him come to me." Even after he did go to Elisha's house and was given ridiculous advice—"Go, wash yourself seven times in the Jordan" (2 Kings 5:10)—Naaman reasoned that the rivers in his own land were "better than any of the waters of Israel" (v. 12). But he was not healed until he went to the place God had chosen to work.

> "For my thoughts are not your thoughts, neither are your ways my ways," declares the LORD.
>
> —ISAIAH 55:8

> But God chose the foolish things of the world to shame the wise; God chose the weak things of the world to shame the strong. He chose the lowly things of this world and the despised things—and the things that are not—to nullify the things that are, so that no one may boast before him.
>
> —1 CORINTHIANS 1:27–29

BE WILLING TO ACCEPT A DIFFERENT ANOINTING THAN WHAT YOU LOST.

A return *to* the anointing, not a return *of* the anointing, means that God will decide how to fill our emptiness. We may reason that the only sense of God we will accept is the way we have always known Him. But He may choose to let that wait for a while—perhaps indefinitely.

In my own "return to Jerusalem," this is one of the hardest things I have had to face. To this very day I have not experienced that exact same sense of God—when Jesus was more real to me than anybody else—I once knew. But He has been pleased to show Himself to me equally powerfully—indeed, more so, but in a different way. I still long for what I had. But at the same time I do not question for a moment that what I have found is the same Jesus I previously experienced!

Early in my ministry at the Westminster Chapel when those visits with Dr. Lloyd-Jones gave me a hunger for the old intimacy with the Lord, I assumed that the same exact feeling would immediately return to me if I quickly put my house in order. I admit to "tokens" and "tastes" now and then, but so far it is *not* what I once felt. And yet, for all I know, God probably works through me today in a way He could not have done then. I have had to be content with a different anointing—one that is maintained by a continual spirit of dignifying trials and totally forgiving others. I only know that I would not exchange anything in this world for what I now have. And if I am totally honest, I prefer what I now have to what I previously lost. At the same time, I do not deny that I'd love to have the same old feeling as well.

ACCEPT AN ANOINTING DIFFERENT FROM WHAT YOU MAY EXPECT OR SEEK.

When we lose the special presence of the Dove—whether by grieving Him or because God sovereignly "stays behind" as we move on—we forfeit any "right" to demand the return of the same anointing. We must be willing to adjust to the way God chooses to manifest His glory, should He be gracious to do so.

Joseph and Mary were desperate. Although they were upset when they found Jesus showing His glory in an unexpected way, they were not going to walk away from Him!

You may have been seeking the Lord, but not with the openness to the Spirit that you thought was required. Be willing to take God any way you find Him, seek Him with all your heart and be willing to adjust to any aspect or measure of His glory that He is willing to unveil.

The forgotten anointing also consists of hidden ways God speaks and acts that nobody has yet experienced. What if God were to show up to *you* in a way He hadn't done to those you respected most? What if He shows up in your life in a way He didn't do with Athanasias, Luther, Calvin, Wesley or your present hero? Will you still welcome Him?

When the psalmist speaks of God confiding in those who fear Him, which the King James Version terms "the secret of the LORD" (Ps. 25:14), you must expect the Lord to tell you anything! You may also be required to keep quiet about it! This is why it is a secret and why He confides. He may have in mind a special relationship with you that nobody else on earth has. Were that to be the case, you can be quite certain you will be required to keep it to yourself until you get to heaven. If you say, "That wouldn't be fun if I couldn't tell it," this privilege will not be offered.

God is seeking those who seek Him with such openness that He can be Himself to that person in a way He cannot be to others. He is a jealous God and looks for one who is happy for God to be the only person who knows what is happening to you. (See John 5:44.) This means a willingness to accept an anointing that is different from what you expect or seek.

ACCEPT HIS GENTLE REBUKE WHEN HE IS FOUND.

Jesus' response to His parents was, "Didn't you know I had to be in my Father's house?" (Luke 2:49). As Calvin put it, "Christ is right to reprove His mother, though He does so with restraint and indirectly." Jesus would not break a bruised reed (Matt. 12:20). Both Joseph and Mary were bruised reeds by this time. They needed a rebuke, but how gentle it was!

When we return to the anointing we may expect a rebuke. But it is always tender. Job's words "How faint the whisper" (Job 26:14) perfectly describe the way God often speaks. The Holy Spirit's sensitivity to us results in tremendous peace and calm when we are sensitive to

Him. God manifested Himself to Elijah in a new way—it was not in the wind, the earthquake or fire, but "a gentle whisper" (1 Kings 19:12). It is the way you and I are advised to approach another person who has been overtaken in a sin (Gal. 6:1). When we are harsh and judgmental, we are not mirroring the Spirit of Jesus.

The unveiling of God's glory is usually characterized by a rebuke and exposure of some weakness or sin. This is how we grow. I have talked to many people (and hear of many others) who learned lessons from the Lord "on the floor" when they fell after being prayed for. My wife, Louise, is a good example. While attending meetings conducted by Rodney Howard-Browne in Florida in January 1995, she called me to say, "It is the greatest thing that has ever happened to me, the nearest you get to heaven without dying." She spent hours on the carpet listening to and *learning* from the Lord. Her chief concern when she came back to London was, "I don't want to lose this." It has changed her life.

A return to the anointing, then, will almost certainly mean hearing something from God that amounts to a rebuke. Why? We all need to change. Joseph and Mary needed to change.

ACCEPT TRUTH YOU MAY NOT WISH WAS TRUE.

Jesus asked, "Didn't you know I had to be in my Father's house?" He was lovingly confronting His parents with the truth they didn't want to hear. Calvin said, "The wonder is that Joseph and Mary did not understand this reply." They knew better than anyone the truth about Jesus.

The unfolding of God's glory is also the unfolding of truth. This may mean truth we haven't wanted fully to accept—at least not yet.

This can be exceedingly difficult for those in leadership,

especially if we have espoused teaching that we may have to abandon. It is harder if we have to accept teaching we had opposed, and harder still if we have gone to print—and have to retract! I have had to do so, but the inner peace and joy far outweighs the fear of criticism that may or may not follow.

Jesus said, "If anyone chooses to do God's will, he will find out whether my teaching comes from God or whether I speak on my own" (John 7:17). That means if I am obedient I will come to truth and can be preserved from grievous error. But if that truth is right there before my eyes, but I can't bear the thought of embracing it, my prayer for an ever-increasing anointing is not sincere.

There are thousands of doctrines taught by Christians that often contradict each other. This can only mean they aren't all correct. At some time, somebody moved ahead without Jesus and took a following with him. I am not so naive as to believe that all of us who desire a greater anointing will be able to sign our names to each other's theology. We must be true to ourselves. But at the same time it is surely not good that some Christians can oppose each other on some of the most fundamental teachings of God's Word.

ACCEPT BEING PUT IN YOUR PLACE.

That is exactly what happened to Joseph and Mary. All of us can expect this to happen to us when we rediscover the special presence of God. Why? Well, to keep us from taking ourselves too seriously.

Joseph and Mary not only focused on themselves, but they also felt that God owed them something. Rather than being thrilled that they found Jesus, they were angry. They possibly felt betrayed. They now took it personally that Jesus was perfectly at home in the temple courts with the teachers of the Law and not with them. They didn't

195

want God to be God. They wanted to maintain control.

The return to the anointing means a total surrender of control. This means we affirm God's own opinion. In one sense, we may rightly refer to *our* anointing. But at the end of the day, it is not ours—it is His. It is "on loan," as it were. We must therefore respect it and never forget that we can lose it again. We lose it when we try to control.

Joseph and Mary had lost control and wanted it back. But Jesus' question, "Didn't you know I had to be in my Father's house?", helped them to accept their place.

> Do not be quick with your mouth,
> > do not be hasty in your heart
> > to utter anything before God.
> God is in heaven
> > and you are on earth,
> > so let your words be few.
> > —ECCLESIASTES 5:2

196

I imagine that Jesus' soft question to His parents was in private. Luke does not specifically say this, but it seems likely that Jesus put this to them when the three of them went off to one side. Jesus has a way of letting us save face. Most of the time, Jesus does not put us in our place by embarrassing us before people looking on. He kindly teaches us a lesson we will never forget by showing us our folly in secret. Even when the public proclamation of the Word exposes someone, no one but God really knows what is taking place inside that person's heart.

MISUNDERSTANDING THE OBVIOUS

"But they did not understand what he was saying to them" (Luke 2:50). They should have, but they didn't. A return to the anointing will bring us face to face with things we cannot fully grasp. Usually we have not seen all of the implications of what we have once been taught. As we have seen, Joseph and Mary knew more than anybody the truth as to Jesus' origin. But they still didn't understand His statement about having to be in His Father's house. Joseph should have known that Jesus wasn't referring to him, but to God the Father.

Jesus' style of asking questions years later was not entirely unlike His question to Joseph and Mary. He had a way of asking a question that might have tended to make one feel a bit stupid—but it was always done to rebuke unbelief. For example, when Jesus enabled Peter to walk on the water, all went well until Peter saw the wind. He cried out to be saved as he began to sink. "Immediately Jesus reached out his hand and caught him. 'You of little faith,' he said, *why did you doubt?*'" (Matt. 14:31, emphasis added).

On another occasion, when asked about the parable of the sower, Jesus said to His disciples, "Don't you understand *this* parable?" It's as though He were saying, "This is an easy one; how then will you understand any parable?" (See Mark 4:13.) He did not really do this to make them feel stupid. He wanted to force them to look again at what He had just said. Then they would conclude for themselves what He felt was obvious.

This is true with any manifestation of God's glory. At first our reaction may be bewilderment. But looking again in the light of what we have already learned will reveal that there is a credible explanation for what God chooses to do.

FOCUS ON CHRIST'S GLORY.

The ultimate reason for the return to the anointing—and for any manifestation of God's glory—is that God will be the main attraction. That was the permanent lesson in this story of Joseph and Mary finding Jesus in the temple. He held center stage!

197

> I am the LORD; that is my name!
> I will not give my glory to another.

> —ISAIAH 42:8

I suspect that all delays to seeing God's glory manifested are partly explained by an unconscious desire in us to have a share of the glory in what God does. I doubt there is such a thing as an unmixed motive. We may tell ourselves that our prayer for revival is entirely for God's honor. We may feel the same way over wanting a greater anointing, that it is only for His sake. We may think we truly mean that.

But one thing is certain: When and where God does show up, He will come in such a manner that no one will think his or her own actions brought God's glory. God will turn up in such a way that He gets total credit.

> It is not for your sake, O house of Israel, that I am going to do these things, but for the sake of my holy name.

> —EZEKIEL 36:22

198

The moment any of us elbows in on God's territory, one of two things will follow:

- He will back off entirely, or

- We will be removed from the picture. "So that no one may boast before him" (1 Cor. 1:29).

God is sensitive about His own honor, and the Holy Spirit mirrors that sensitivity. Adjustment to Him means forfeiting any control or credit in order that He remain in our midst—as the Dove remained on Jesus.

CONCLUSION

> Then he went down to Nazareth with them and was obedient to them. But his mother treasured all these things in her heart.
>
> —Luke 2:51

Do you believe that you are consciously in the will of God? God wants us to be in His will and to know what His will is. Paul exhorted us to "understand what the Lord's will is" (Eph. 5:17). Paul's word followed the previous admonition: "Find out what pleases the Lord" (v. 10). When we find out what pleases the Lord—and then do it—we may be sure that we are in His will.

The inner testimony of the Spirit, which will always correspond to God's revealed will (the Bible), is sufficient to convey that we are in His will. If we are not in His will it is because we either didn't obey God's explicit Word, like Jonah (Jon. 1:1–3), or we moved ahead of Him, like Joseph and Mary.

But "all's well that ends well," as Shakespeare put it. In the case of Jonah, God came to him a second time, and he obeyed (Jon. 3:1–3). At the end of the day, after having had a quarrel with the Lord, Jonah let God have the last word (Jon. 4:11).

All ended well for Samson, too. He accomplished more at the end of his life "than while he lived" (Judg. 16:30).

So it was with Joseph and Mary. All three of the above accounts have these ingredients in common—the people referred to were temporarily out of God's will but fully in it in the end. Is it possible to be out of the will of God and yet in the will of God at the same time? Yes. God permits things in our lives that sidetrack us for a time. But it is part of His long-term strategy for our lives. All that is permitted as to time and circumstance is redeemable. In other words, God helps us to buy back time—He repays us for the years the locusts have eaten (Joel 2:25).

> And we know that all things work together for good
> to them that love God, to them who are the called
> according to his purpose.
>
> —ROMANS 8:28, KJV

Samson developed a sensitivity to the Spirit during the time "the hair on his head began to grow again after it had been shaved" (Judg. 16:22). Whether one has sinned grievously like Samson or has run ahead of the Lord like Joseph and Mary, God does not desert His own. His aim in each case is to teach us His "ways"—if we will listen. As long as we can hear God's voice and accept His rebukes, it means we are not stone deaf to the Spirit. Not only is God not finished with us, but the best is around the corner.

Knowing God's ways comes from developing an ever-increasing sensitivity to His Spirit. This is a most gracious invitation—never turn down an opportunity like this!

Joseph and Mary made the adjustment to Jesus, and their relationship thereafter was richer than ever. For certain they had a respect for the Son of God greater than before. Once we return to the anointing, we have a reverence and appreciation for it that helps ensure we don't repeat past mistakes.

We can learn from Jesus' example, too. He submitted to His parents in accordance with the Law (Exod. 20:12) and His mission to fulfill it (Matt. 5:17). His obedience was an act of humility for our salvation. "He fulfilled God's intentions," says Calvin, "that for a time He should shelter under Joseph's name, as under a shadow... All the more freely should we, each of us, undergo the yoke which the Lord may lay upon our necks."

Jesus was sensitive to the Spirit when He stayed behind in Jerusalem, and He continued to be sensitive to the Spirit by submitting to His parents. This was still true in His life and ministry years later. Paul's epistle to the Romans tells us that He "did not please himself" (Rom. 15:3). All sensitivity to the Spirit, of which Jesus was the supreme example, consists in our not pleasing ourselves.

The yoke that the Lord may lay upon our necks is to be welcomed. It is the best way to live. Jesus invited us to learn from Him that we may find rest for our souls, for His yoke is easy and His burden is light (Matt. 11:29–30).

May the blessing of God Almighty be upon you.

NOTES

CHAPTER ONE: THE SENSITIVITY
OF THE HEAVENLY DOVE

1. "Like a River Glorious" by Frances R. Havergal (1836–1879). Public domain.
2. R. T. Kendall, *The Anointing: Yesterday, Today, Tomorrow* (London: Hodder and Stoughton, 2001). In our book I included the following quote from our friend Pete Cantrell: "The greatest freedom is having nothing to prove."
3. Although doves and pigeons are in the same scientific order of birds as pigeons, there seems to be no empirical studies on their temperaments. The focus of scientific investigation centers mainly on their origins, locations, sizes, color and feeding habits.
4. The so-called London pigeons in Trafalgar Square, like the pigeons that flock in every city center, are called *feral pigeons*. *Peristera* is the Greek word for "dove;" *trygon* is the word for "turtledove." Many theologians relate the reference to the turtledove in Song of Solomon 2:12 to the Holy Spirit. The ancient Hebrew scholar Philo saw the dove as a symbol of the *logos* (word), the *nous* (mind) or *sophia* (wisdom). The New International Version of Song of Solomon 2:12 ("the cooing of doves") does not reflect that the word *turtledoves* is meant in the original language. Yet the general word for *dove* may well imply *turtledove* in most cases in either the Old or the New Testament, even if the specific word for turtledove is not used.
5. "Send the Fire" by William Booth (1829–1912), founder of the Salvation Army. Public domain.
6. I have fully described this experience in my book *The Anointing: Yesterday, Today, Tomorrow.*

CHAPTER FOUR: WHY IS GOD SOMETIMES SILENT?

1. Robert Burns, "To a Louse," written after Burns observed a louse crawling about on a lady's bonnet in church one day.
2. "Green Fields 127" by John Newton (1725–1807). Public domain.
3. The "Toronto Blessing" is the name given by the *Sunday Telegraph* when describing the phenomenon of falling down and laughing, either after being prayed for or through the laying on of hands. I initially had grave doubts, but eventually accepted it as a genuine move of the Spirit. I have been criticized for my stand, because many thought it would lead me away from my ministry of expository preaching. We did lose twenty members, and no doubt more who regularly attended Westminster Chapel. It made me sensitive to my critics, who felt that the Toronto Blessing would replace the importance of preaching.

CHAPTER SIX: HOW WE CAN BECOME INSENSITIVE TO THE SPIRIT

1. "Did You Think to Pray" by Mary A. Kidder (1820–1905). Public domain.
2. "What a Friend We Have in Jesus" by Joseph Medlicott Scriven (1819–1886). Public domain.

CHAPTER SEVEN: RECOGNIZING GOD'S ABSENCE

1. "Wonderful, Wonderful, Jesus Is to Me" by Haldor Lillenas (1885–1959), copyright © 1924, renewed 1951 by Lillenas Publishing Company, admin. by The Copyright Company. All rights reserved. Used by permission.

CHAPTER EIGHT: PIGEON RELIGION

1. Generally speaking, a Calvinist believes in predestination and the eternal security of the believer. For more information, see my book *Calvin and English Calvinism to 1649* (Carlisle, Cumbris, UK: Paternoster, 1979, 1997).

CHAPTER NINE: THE ROAD BACK

1. "Like a River Glorious" by Frances R. Havergal (1836–1879). Public domain.
2. The details that led to my friend's statement to me can be found in my book *God Meant It for Good* (Carlisle, Cumbris, UK: Paternoster, 1986).
3. Some of the events that have contributed to a greater anointing are described in my book *The Anointing: Yesterday, Today, Tomorrow*.

FOR EVERYONE WHO NEEDS A SECOND CHANCE

From Jonah to the apostle Paul, the great heroes of the Bible had times in their life when they were not so great...not so heroic. Fortunately for us, their stories don't end with their mistakes.

God Gives Second Chances offers you the hope that you too can turn your life around TODAY for the glory of God!

978-1-59979-253-8 / $14.99

GOD GIVES SECOND CHANCES

HOW TO GET UP, DUST OFF AND BE USED AGAIN BY GOD WHEN YOU FALL

R. T. KENDALL

Best-selling author of Total Forgiveness

CHARISMA HOUSE

Visit your local bookstore.

10795

FOR EVERYONE
WHO NEEDS A
SECOND CHANCE
GOD GIVES

From Jonah to the apostle
Paul, the great heroes of
the Bible had messed up their
life when they were not
so great... but so heroic.
Fortunately for us, their
stories connect with their
mistakes.

...God Gives Second Chances
offers you the hope that
you too can turn your life
around GOD's way for the
glory of God.

Visit your local bookstore.

CHARISMA
HOUSE

www.ingramcontent.com/pod-product-compliance
Lightning Source LLC
Chambersburg PA
CBHW010235100426
42812CB00009B/2461